M000308278

Passions

GIACOMO LEOPARDI

TRANSLATED BY TIM PARKS

YALE UNIVERSITY PRESS ■ NEW HAVEN & LONDON

A MARGELLOS
WORLD REPUBLIC OF LETTERS BOOK

The Margellos World Republic of Letters is dedicated to making literary works from around the globe available in English through translation. It brings to the English-speaking world the work of leading poets, novelists, essayists, philosophers, and playwrights from Europe, Latin America, Africa, Asia, and the Middle East to stimulate international discourse and creative exchange.

English translation and introduction copyright © 2014 by Tim Parks.
All rights reserved.

This book may not be reproduced, in whole or in part, including illustrations, in any form (beyond that copying permitted by Sections 107 and 108 of the U.S. Copyright Law and except by reviewers for the public press), without written permission from the publishers.

This book was originally published in Italy by Donzelli Editore under the title *Le passioni*. For the Thematic Edition of the ZIBALDONE DEI PENSIERI. IL TRATTATO DELLE PASSIONI by Giacomo Leopardi, edited by Fabiana Cacciapuoti: **Copyright © 1997–2003–2010 Donzelli Editore.**

Yale University Press books may be purchased in quantity for educational, business, or promotional use. For information, please e-mail sales.press@yale.edu (U.S. office) or sales@yaleup.co.uk (U.K. office).

Set in Electra and Nobel type by Tseng Information Systems, Inc.
Printed in the United States of America.

Page 202 constitutes a continuation of the copyright page.

CONTENTS

In 1817 in the small central Italian town of Recanati, some ten kilometers from the Adriatic coast, a nineteen-year-old hunchback began a notebook with the words "Palazzo Bello. Cane di notte dal casolare, al passare del viandante": Dog in the night from the farmhouse, as the wayfarer passes. Palazzo Bello was the house of family friends, but the note proceeds with the translation (from Latin) of a stanza from Avianus, a fifth-century writer of fables, then goes on to tell the story of a wolf who ingenuously wastes his day hoping to eat a child whose mother has threatened to feed it to the wolves if it doesn't stop crying. The child stops crying, but the mother wouldn't have fed it to the wolf anyway. The page continues with a wry comment on a young man (the writer of the notebook?) whose poetry, full of archaic terms, remains largely incomprehensible to the elderly lady who reads it because "those were not words that were used in her day," to which he replies that he'd thought they were used precisely because very old. In short, this is a world of misunderstandings, frustrations, and uncertain communication, of rapid shifts between familiar surroundings, drawing room anecdote, and antique literature, and above all of language that won't stay still.

The next two entries, taking us into page two, offer first a potted history of literature from "nothing" through "truth" to "refinement," the last being rapidly equated with "corruption." Unfortunately, "there is no example of a return from refinement to truth." Fifteen years and four-and-a-half thousand pages later the notebook closes with five brief entries which include the following remarks:

> People's attitude to life is the same as the Italian husband's toward his wife: he needs to believe she is faithful even though he knows it's not true.

A conflicted psychological state is posited where one knows, but chooses not to know, because knowledge is neither helpful nor attractive. Given the ever-present danger of disillusionment, denial is the default.

> Two truths that most men will never believe: one that we know nothing, the other that we are nothing. Add the third, which depends a lot on the second: that there is nothing to hope for after death.

One might have thought this was knowledge enough, but the final entry, focused as ever on a tension between reality and belief that has now been plumbed and explored in every possible depth and nuance, explodes the last and most resistant bolt hole of all: the idea that, despite all one knows, one's own life might nevertheless prove an exception to the rule:

> The most unexpected thing for someone entering into social life, and very often for someone who has grown old there, is

to find the world as it has been described to him, and as he already knows it and believes it to be in theory. Man is astonished to see that the general rule holds for him too.

This rejection on the writer's part of the idea that he might enjoy a privileged destiny shuts the book with a clunk. The 4,500-plus pages are stacked away in a trunk and passed on, at the hunchback's early death in 1837, to a flamboyant friend, who in turn at his death leaves them, together with other odds and ends, to two housemaids. This in 1888. Eventually, in 1898, publication of what had come to be known as the *Zibaldone* (the word means hotchpotch, or miscellany) began. Today it is considered the greatest intellectual diary of Italian literature, its breadth and depth of thought often compared to the work of Schopenhauer and Nietzsche.

Giacomo Leopardi had not always been ready to accept that he was not an exception to the rule. With good reason. His youth was spent almost entirely in his father's extraordinary library. A minor aristocrat, with an unerring nose for bad business deals, Monaldo Leopardi had been banned by the authorities from handling money, a task taken over by his severe and parsimonious wife, Adelaide. Consoling himself for this loss of power and prestige, Monaldo collected twenty thousand books (in a part of the world where books were hard to come by) and set his firstborn son to reading them. So many of the texts were in foreign languages — the Greek philosophers, the Latin poets and rhetoricians, Madame de Staël, Goethe, Descartes, Montaigne, Rousseau — that Giacomo was more or less obliged to become a prodigy. By age ten he had mastered Latin, Greek, German, and French. Hebrew and English would soon follow. Already his tutors confessed that they had nothing else to teach him. Nor was it merely bookish knowledge. In a fragment of autobiography written in third person in his teens he says this of his younger self:

> The most remarkable, perhaps unique thing about him was that while barely out of boyhood he already had confidence and niceness of discrimination with respect to those great truths that others learn only from experience, this together with an almost complete knowledge of the world and himself, so that he knew all his good and bad traits and the way his nature was developing and was always a step ahead of his own progress.

There was a price to pay for this precocity. Archconservative and papal loyalist, Monaldo had invested heavily in the idea of his son becoming a great Christian apologist. That was the purpose behind those interminable hours of study (much of the library was made up of books bought from the religious institutions that Napoleon had closed). That was why Giacomo received the tonsure at twelve and for a while dressed in a cassock. He was to become a priest. Dutifully, through his teens, amid endless translations and ambitious projects to produce new, philologically accurate editions of various classical authors, he wrote an *Essay on the Popular Errors of the Ancients,* initially aimed at cataloguing and demonstrating the falseness of early pagan beliefs. But while on the one hand Giacomo began to find the ancients' "errors" more attractive than the knowledge and Christian reason that exploded them, on the other, looking in the mirror, he saw a young man whose back, ruined by "seven years of mad and desperate study," had developed a hunch. Obliged by frequent illness to pass his right of inheritance, as first-born, to his younger brother, troubled by constant problems with his eyes, frail and almost grotesque, Giacomo saw before him a life without physical love or financial independence. Studying was the one thing he knew how to do, but the knowledge so gained only revealed to him that knowledge does not help us to live; on the contrary it corrodes those happy errors, or illusions, as he came to call them, that give life meaning, shifting energy to the mental and rational and away from the physical and instinctive, where, in complicity with illusion, happiness lies.

In a later biography of his son, Monaldo wrote of Giacomo in this period that "setting himself to thinking about how one breathes," he found that he could no longer breathe; "thinking and ruminating on the act of urination," he was no longer able to urinate. "Thought," Giacomo wrote in a letter in his early twenties, "can crucify and torment a person."

This paradox of the brilliant scholar not only disillusioned with reason but determined to use reason to show the limits and perversity of reason would run through all Leopardi's work. The one area that seemed capable of reconciling the destructively antithetical energies at work here, hence saving Giacomo from himself, was poetry. As a boy, he had despised it as nonrational. Later it was precisely the instinctive quality of poetry, its arising from natural impulses, from sound and song rather than from reasoning and research, that he prized.

Only poets inspire in me a burning desire to translate and
take hold of what I read; and only nature and emotions
inspire that violent, restless urge to compose . . .

But even poetry offered only a consolation of "half an hour";
afterward Leopardi was back with the grim reality of poor health,
poor eyesight, a father determined to keep him under his conserva-
tive thumb, a mother whose rigid Christianity and obsession with
domestic finance stifled all natural affection, and a home remote
from any center of culture or kindred spirit. It was in his late teens,
as Leopardi became fully aware of this unhappy condition, that he
began to write the *Zibaldone*. Remarkably, it is not primarily self-
referential and never self-pitying. Rather, it brings together his wide
reading and remarkable powers of observation to focus on the question: how did man get to be what he now is, a confusion of vital
animal instinct and mortifying reason, of nature and civilization?
Here, for example, is how the very personal issue of his mother is
drawn into an ongoing consideration of the fatal alliance between
Christianity and reason:

> The extent to which Christianity is contrary to nature, when
> it acts solely on simple, rigid reasoning and when this is taken
> as the sole norm for behavior, can be seen from the following
> example. I once knew very well the mother of a family who
> was not in the least superstitious, but devout and unswerving
> in her Christian faith and in the practice of her religion. She
> not only felt no sympathy for parents who lost their children
> in infancy but positively and sincerely envied them, because
> such infants had flown safe and sound straight to paradise,

and had freed their parents from the inconvenience of sup-
porting them. Finding herself more than once in danger of
losing her own children at the same age, she did not ask God
to let them die, because her religion forbade this, but she
rejoiced with all her heart . . .

One says of the *Zibaldone* that it is a notebook, but it was begun
as and for the most part continued as a bundle of loose pages. Leopardi had no idea how long it would be or what would be the principles of its organization. Again, one says that it was written over
fifteen years, but Leopardi had already passed four thousand pages
at the end of 1823, less than six years after beginning, and would
add only another five hundred in the next nine. In 1820 he began
to add a date to every entry, suggesting an awareness that his views
were changing, and from 1821 to 1823, between the ages of twenty-
three and twenty-five, he wrote more than three thousand pages,
two-thirds of the whole. What we are looking at, then, is the work
of a young man widely read but entirely untraveled and socially inexperienced, who is seeking to throw off the shackles of his parents'
religion and aspirations for him but has nowhere to take his energies and investigations, nowhere to forge his identity, if not on the
pages of this notebook; here he debates urgently with Rousseau and
Vico, Plato and Aristotle, Machiavelli and Bruno, setting up a grill
of oppositions (nature / culture, animal / human, ancient / modern, male / female, childhood / adulthood) in which all experience
is tested and placed; weighing up the irreversible nature of the civilizing process against notions of circularity, return, and repetition.
Aware that the world of ideas is in constant flux, he explores the

origins of words and grammatical structures in a dozen languages, tracking linguistic development against cultural refinement.

All these studies are then measured against personal experience, or alternatively an intense experience will prompt him to look for help from his books. One of his key discoveries, as early as 1819, arises not out of study but out of intense boredom. For if beliefs and illusions foster activity and excitement, which are always a pleasure, the deconstruction of those beliefs leads to inertia and unhappiness. And if Christianity and reason together had swept away all the illusions that drove human activity in ancient times, one needed only to go a step further and dismiss the Christian God to be left with nothing at all. In a rare, brief, personal entry, Giacomo writes:

> I was frightened to find myself in the midst of nothingness, a nothing myself. I felt as if I were suffocating, thinking and feeling that all is nothing, solid nothing.

> In such circumstances

> it could be said that there will never be heroic, generous, and sublime action, or high thoughts and feelings, that are anything more than real and genuine illusions, and whose price must fall as the empire of reason increases.

It is because Leopardi believes that such "genuine illusions" can be constructed only "in words" that the *Zibaldone* focuses so frequently on language, on etymology, on the relationship between languages and the processes by which each language changes, gradually shifting toward a more intellectual, uniform, codified vision of the world.

Everything strange and unusual . . . that modern travelers
see and report in the customs and habits of civilized nations
is nothing other than what remains of their ancient institutions. . . . But they certainly won't find anything strange or
unusual in what is modern. . . . Aside from some small differences arising from climate and national character, differences
that are increasingly giving way to the modern impulse to be
alike in everything, . . . everywhere, and especially among
the cultured classes, people are taking care to distance themselves from everything that is unusual and peculiar to their
own national customs, seeking no other distinction than to
resemble the rest of mankind as much as they can. And in
general one could say that the modern spirit tends to reduce
the whole world to one nation, and all nations to a single
person. . . . Even language is becoming uniform these days,
thanks to the extraordinarily wide use of French, something
I don't object to when it comes to usefulness, but that I definitely do when it's a question of beauty.

The proper purpose of study, given this "antinatural, modern
life," was to unlearn the habits of mind and expression that over
the preceding centuries had come to seem natural and to try to
get back to a more immediate apprehension of the world's and our
own true nature, even if there could never be any question of returning to a previous state. The *Zibaldone* thus begins to assume
the tone of an across-the-board attack on received wisdom, notions
of progress, and pieties of every kind. Seeking to isolate the springs
of such emotions as compassion or envy, Leopardi makes a dis-

tinction between self-love or self-regard on the one hand and egoism or self-centeredness on the other. A high level of self-regard,
which comes naturally to the person who is young and healthy and
lives in a society that collectively thinks well of itself, predisposes
a person toward compassion and charity that, in turn, reinforce
his self-regard. But the person whose self-regard has been undermined by ill health, old age, failure, disillusionment, or a society,
such as Italy's, which has a poor opinion of itself, retreats into self-
centeredness; in trouble or danger, he will defend himself and his
own interests at all costs, careless of the destiny of even those closest
to him. Another's troubles make no impression on him while another's success is a motive for envy. Paradoxically, while self-regard
makes compassion possible, it also naturally leads to an underlying
hatred of our fellow man.

> The sight of a happy man, full of some good luck he's had . . .
> is almost always extremely irksome . . . so that the man who
> has reason to be happy will either have to hide his pleasure, or
> be casual and amusing about it, as if it hardly mattered, other-
> wise his presence and conversation will prove hateful and
> tiresome. . . . What can all this mean but that our self-regard
> inevitably and without our noticing leads us to hate our fel-
> low man?

What is striking is Leopardi's absolutely unblinkered attention
to every nuance of emotion in almost every imaginable social situation. He comes back and back to the questions of envy and compassion, in particular their aesthetic or sexual component (how much
easier it is to feel compassion for a pretty girl rather than for an ugly

old man); he considers a huge range of situations, showing how a person's behavior and thinking changes in relation to the illusions or hopes he or she is able to sustain, or the disappointments he or she has suffered; he delves into the question of how aesthetic responses alter over the centuries, compelling us to acknowledge the relative nature of more or less any knowledge or judgment. And all this is done with a quiet insistence that draws every eventuality into a general sense of scandal at the distance between the real nature of experience and the way it is ordinarily described. Here he is tackling the comforts offered by Christianity:

> The promise and expectation of a very great happiness but that, 1., man cannot understand, nor imagine, nor conceive of . . ., 2., that he well knows he will never be able to conceive of, nor imagine, nor have any idea about his lifelong and, 3., that he knows very well is of a completely different nature from and alien to the happiness he desires in this world . . . such a promise . . . is really not of a kind to console an unhappy and unfortunate man in this life. . . . The happiness man naturally desires is a temporal happiness, a material happiness, something to be experienced through the senses and by our minds as they are now and as we experience them; in short, a happiness of this life and this existence, not of another life and another existence that we know must be entirely different from this one, and that we cannot conceive of and don't know what qualities it's made up of.

Reading and rereading what he had written provoked new lines of thought, new attempts to bring all human behavior into a scheme that saw man declining in relation to the now "preponderant and overwhelming" supremacy of the rational faculty. Elements of the *Zibaldone* then reemerged in the poetry he had begun to write in rare sporadic bursts, lyrics that could not be farther in tone from the knotted, cumulative prose of the *Zibaldone* but that fit in with the belief that what is finest in human expression is what arises most immediately from an intense unmediated engagement with the world and is then expressed simply and directly. Here is the celebrated *L'infinito*, written in 1818. The central idea of the poem, that the mind finds repose not in knowledge but in everything it cannot know or see but only imagine, is central to the thrust of the *Zibaldone*.

> It was always a favorite of mine,
> This lonely hill and the hedge
> In front that hides so much
> Of the distant horizon. But sitting,
> Gazing, my mind goes beyond
> That barrier, to conjure endless
> Spaces there and deep deep stillness
> Till my heart shudders. And
> Hearing the wind rustle in these leaves,
> I start comparing that infinite silence
> With this voice close by; and I think
> Of eternity and seasons past, and
> Of here, now, alive, how it feels.
> So my thoughts sink in this immensity
> And I find pleasure drowning in this deep sea.

Aged twenty-four, Leopardi finally left home to live in Rome, but returned to Recanati in a matter of months, defeated and disgusted both with Roman society and with his own timidity. How mad it was, he reflected, that a man whose pessimism and despair led him to welcome the thought of death was nevertheless afraid of making a fool of himself in company, and this "out of a fear of making life worse, when actually he no longer cares about life anyway."

Later, Leopardi spent periods in Milan, Bologna, and Florence, always in the hope of finding some remunerative literary employment that never materialized, frequently falling in love with women who were not even remotely available to him. In his travels — "a walking sepulcher," he called himself — from one temporary lodging to another, the *Zibaldone* was always beside him, transforming disappointment into reflection. It was extraordinary, he remarked, how hope and illusion would return even when one knew perfectly well they could lead to nothing; on the other hand, why not interest oneself in the most frivolous things if life in general was meaningless. Again and again depression led to sudden flowerings of what is now thought some of the finest poetry ever written in Italian, though in his lifetime it brought him little recognition and no wealth. The same was true of the uncannily lucid *Operette Morali* (1827), a series of prose dialogues between mythical and historical figures that drew on material in the *Zibaldone* to express the human condition as essentially comic. Considering the *Operette*, unfavorably, for the Accademia della Crusca's annual literary prize, one member of the jury complained that far from being moral, the dialogues undermined every basis for morality.

Merely to list the subjects Leopardi tackles in the *Zibaldone* would take up many pages. So many of his intuitions look forward to the work of future philosophers, to absurdism and existentialism; again and again the voices of Nietzsche, Dostoevsky, Wittgenstein, Gadda, Beckett, Bernhard, Cioran, and many others seem to murmur on the page. We are told that there is no point in speaking of things that cannot be known; that any meaning attributed to life is a product of the imagination and hence precarious, and infinitely more so once we become aware of this fact; above all, we are warned that

> those innumerable and immense questions about time and space, argued over from the beginnings of metaphysics onward . . . are none other than wars of words, caused by misunderstandings, and imprecision of thought, and limited ability to understand our mind, which is the only place where time and space, like many other abstract things, exist independently and for themselves.

One consequence of these conclusions was the impossibility of turning his *Zibaldone* into a comprehensive system of philosophy, since any illusion of the objectivity required to achieve such a thing was long gone. Hence the complete edition of the work is not a book one reads through from start to finish, but an endless pleasure garden for browsing and reflection. Leopardi became aware of this relation between the pessimism of his thinking and the eventual form of his work early on, and in 1827 he began to index and cross-reference the vast collection of loose pages to allow them to be approached thematically rather than read through. Using 550 tiny slips of paper, he first established an index of many hundreds of entries, then identified a smaller number of general themes whose occurrence he tracked throughout the book. These include such things as "Civilization. Process of Civilization," "Pleasure. Theory of Pleasure," "Manual of Practical Philosophy," "Memories of My Life." There are indications in his letters that he was considering extracting material from the *Zibaldone* to make up separate and more manageable books on these themes. One was to be entitled "Treatise on the Passions, Human Qualities, etc.," and it is from the 164 entries referenced under this heading that the present book is made up.

By passions, Leopardi means emotions, sentiment, feeling, the whole range of mental activity that is not purely intellectual and rational but rather reminds us of the indissolubility of mind and body. In a natural state, he supposes, mind and body would be in harmony and feelings direct, simple and strong, openly expressed and quickly forgotten. The extraordinary complexity and contortedness of modern man's feelings, then, their smoldering, chronic self-destructiveness, which is the real subject of this book, becomes an index of how far the civilizing process has altered man's emotional life, made it at once subtler, more nuanced, and infinitely unhappier. For example, each of the entries in this book is headed with indications of the other themes under which the same passage is referenced. One of the most frequent of these is "Social Machiavellianism." Entries under this heading will suggest how living in society has taught us to mask our feelings and proceed indirectly to our goals, something that then tends to dull the passions and make them more elusive, tortuous, and durable, because never openly expressed. A long and fascinating entry on "the spiritualization of love" discusses the way an increasing focus on the hidden, mental, or spiritual qualities of the beloved, rather than a frank attention to the physical, has profoundly altered what might have appeared to be the most natural and animal of the passions, creating that infinitely pleasurable, but strangely comic, even grotesque phenomenon that is sentimental love. On occasion Leopardi lets another writer do his job, simply quoting a passage that furthers his argument. Here he is, for example, quoting Antoine-Léonard Thomas on the way Christianity altered female sexuality:

> It's easy to see the prodigious revolution that this era inevitably brought with it in people's habits. The women, almost all of lively imagination and fervent spirit, gave themselves over to virtue and the more suffering was involved the better they felt about it. They find just as much happiness overcoming a grand passion as satisfying it. The soul takes pleasure in its efforts and as long as it is making an effort it hardly matters if that effort is being made against itself.

Aside from the pungency and eloquence of Leopardi's thinking, the passages are held together by our growing feeling that what we are reading is a strong and disturbing narrative, a story that remorselessly pieces together for us the inevitable destiny of the intelligent and sensitive man born into the modern era and hence doomed to live in a world where the demands of society limit the range of vigorous, satisfying external action, turning the mind inward, where Christianity first and atheism later offer no superhuman force we might blame for our unhappiness (as the ancients could blame the gods), prompting a constant experience of anxiety and guilt around our dissatisfactions, as if they were somehow our fault, and in extreme cases first self-hatred in the face of failure, and ultimately, if one is not destroyed by self-hatred, a fatal indifference to everybody and everything caused by an irretrievable loss of self-regard. Without giving details or seeking sympathy, Leopardi lets us know that he has been through the process he describes.

> For myself, every time I have been convinced of the inevita-
> bility and permanence of my misery . . . I found myself nur-
> turing a furious hatred against myself, because the misery I
> hated was located nowhere but in myself; so I was the only
> possible object of my hatred, since I had no one else, recog-
> nized no one else whom I could blame for my troubles and
> no one else who could become a target of my hatred for
> this reason. I conceived a burning desire to take revenge
> on myself and on my own life for a misery that was inevi-
> table and inseparable from my very being, and I experienced
> a fierce joy, a supreme joy, at the thought of suicide. The
> unyielding world clashed with my own unyielding nature,
> and when the collision came—me incapable of giving way,
> easing off, or backing down and the world even less so—the
> loser in the struggle could only be me.

Looking forward to the sort of tormented mental territory de-scribed in Dostoevsky's *Notes from Underground*, or again in a dif-ferent way to T. S. Eliot's "Hollow Men," Leopardi puts together a grim account of a world where the best minds are swiftly defeated and consequently lapse, in early adulthood, into apathy and, anticipating Thoreau, "quiet desperation."

> In fact these days one might say that anyone who has a certain level of intelligence and feeling, having had some experience of the world . . . will fall into this state . . . and stay in it till they die. . . . Ordinarily, people like this are mostly concerned with keeping things as they are, plodding along with their methodical lives, changing nothing, doing nothing new, not because they are fearful or idle—before they fell into this state they'll have been quite the opposite—but out of a reluctance that comes from their experience of adversity and prompts them to fear that any new development would upset this restfulness, quietness, slumber, into which after long struggles and much resistance their spirit has finally fallen, withdrawn, huddled up in itself almost. The world today is full of people living in this . . . kind of desperation. . . . It's not hard then to see just how much the enterprise, variety, mobility, and vitality of this world will stand to gain when all the best minds, I think we can say, on reaching maturity, become incapable of action, and of no use to themselves or to others.

Yet Leopardi's *Passions* is not a depressing book. The energy of the author's analysis, the forthrightness with which he cuts through all the pieties, the uncanny accuracy of his descriptions of how the mind deals with pleasure and pain, hope and fear, love and hate, is always invigorating, stirring, exciting. As he wrote in the early pages of the *Zibaldone*:

> Works of [literary] genius have this intrinsic quality, that
> even when they capture exactly the nothingness of things, or
> vividly reveal and make us feel life's inevitable unhappiness,
> or express the most acute hopelessness . . . they are always a
> source of consolation and renewed enthusiasm.

Indeed, looked at from a different angle, one might consider the whole of Leopardi's work as prompted by the question: how, once we have decided that the world is meaningless and hopeless, can we construct, however temporarily, however precariously, some meaning and some hope for ourselves, since without those qualities life is simply impossible. There is no easy answer to this question; but one strategy for getting by no doubt was precisely this immensely energetic and intricate consideration of the present state of the human soul.

TEXTUAL NOTE

This book is made up of 164 entries extracted from the *Zibaldone*. In 1827, in his eagerness to use the material of what now amounted to more than four thousand handwritten pages to arrive at some profitable publication, Leopardi first indexed the whole work, then established twenty-three separate headings, each of which might form the subject of a separate book. One of these was a "Treatise on the Passions." For each heading he then listed, using page and paragraph numbers, all the entries, or parts of entries, in the *Zibaldone* that touched on those subjects. Inevitably, many entries appear in more than one subject heading. That he had begun to think of some kind of organization for each book beyond a simple accumulation of material is clear from the fact that he does not list the entries in the order in which they were written, although for the most part the general chronology of their production is respected.

In this book, then, we give those entries that Leopardi listed for his treatise on the passions, arranging them in the same order Leopardi listed them. At the beginning of each paragraph, in boldface, we have also indicated the other subject headings, or alphabetical index entries, in which the same paragraph appears. Hence one paragraph might have the entry *Civilization. Process of Civilization—*

Glory. Fame—Of Nature and another *The Ancients—Moral Etiquette—Envy—Social Machiavellianism.* These paragraph "titles" will give the reader a sense of the themes around which Leopardi was seeking to organize his material, the importance for him, for example, of the idea of the civilizing process, its relation to man in a state of nature, the phenomenon of "social Machiavellianism" (the habit of concealing one's feelings in order to achieve a certain end), and so on.

To complicate matters a little, within some of the entries we find cross-references to other entries in the *Zibaldone* that deal with the same subject matter. In these cases we have left Leopardi's reference with the original page number of the *Zibaldone* (all complete editions of the *Zibaldone* use the same page numbers), placed an asterisk beside the number, and introduced the passage referred to beneath the entry where the reference occurs, tagging it with an asterisk. In cases where more than one other entry is referenced we have used further symbols to tag the references. We have keyed these cross-referenced paragraphs with symbols and placed each at the end of the appropriate passage, but they are not footnotes as such, nor is there any question of a hierarchy that might give more importance to one paragraph over another.

What we are reading, then, is a work in progress, and what's more the work of a man who had ceased to believe it was possible to create a comprehensive philosophical system and set it down in impeccable order. Each separate entry stands alone, but each gains from being read alongside the others. Often one feels that Leopardi was groping toward a hypertext structure in which the reader might choose what order he reads in, or which links and cross-references he wishes to follow. Yet within each entry, whether long or short, an eloquent rhetoric prevails revealing a highly disciplined mind, simultaneously aware of the need to organize and the need to be aware of everything that eludes organization.

Passions

Happiness and Sadness

People will already have noticed that just as happiness prompts us to communicate with others (so that even a normally taciturn person will grow talkative when happy, easily falling into conversation with people he would otherwise have avoided or not wanted to speak to, etc.), so sadness leads us to shun society and shrink into ourselves with our own thoughts and distress. Still, I'd like to point out how this tendency to expansiveness in happiness and contraction in sadness also affects a person's movement and gait; when happy he throws out his arms and legs, swinging his hips and opening up, in a way, by moving swiftly back and forth, as though looking for room and space; but when sad he shrinks into himself, his head drops, his arms fold and close on his chest, and he walks slowly, refraining from any movement that might be lively or, as it were, ample. I remember once (I noticed this as it happened) I was sitting down absorbed in happy or at least neutral thoughts; then a sad thought came along and at once my knees, from being relaxed and loosely apart, clamped tight together and my chin, which had been tilted upward, dropped down on my chest.

Satirical Thoughts — Envy — Memories of My Life

I used to think the Capuchins were crazy when they excused themselves for treating their novices badly—something they do with great satisfaction and intense personal pleasure—by saying that they themselves had been treated the same way. Since then experience has taught me that this is a natural feeling; the fact is I had just reached an age to free myself from the trammels of a harsh and extremely strict upbringing, but was still living in my father's house with a brother much younger than myself, but not so young as not to be in full command of all his faculties and foibles, etc. Now, although it was absolutely not something my parents wanted, but simply because the kind of life we were all living together had changed, this brother to a large degree shared our freedoms and enjoyed a lot more comforts and nice little treats than we other children had enjoyed at his age; he also had far fewer duties and re-straints and rules and punishments to bother him than we had had, as a result of which he was much cheekier and more brazen than we were at his age. In natural response I felt a very real envy; I wasn't envious of the privileges he enjoyed, since I now had the same privi-leges myself and could hardly hope now to have them retrospec-tively for the time past; I simply felt irritated that he should have them and wished rather that he be harassed and tormented as we had been. This is pure, unadulterated envy of the worst variety, and I felt it naturally, without wanting to feel it. But I understood then (and that was when I wrote this down) that this is human nature, and I saw how the privileges, whatever they amounted to, that I was now enjoying were becoming less attractive to me because I was sharing them with him; perhaps they no longer seemed a sufficient reward for what I had had to put up with since someone else who was now in the same position I'd once been in, someone less de-serving than myself, had acquired them with no effort at all. Let's apply this to the Capuchins: finding that they hold the fate of their younger brothers, the novices, in their hands, they act on impulses dictated by the inclination I've been describing; they can't bear the idea that the privileges they've acquired be cheapened by allowing others to have them with less trouble than themselves, nor that these youngsters, now in the same circumstances they were once in, not suffer the same tribulations they suffered.

Envy — Memories of My Life

I've never envied anyone for talents I believed I had myself, literary talents, for example; on the contrary, in those cases I've always been more than ready to praise. No, I think I first experienced envy (toward someone very close to me) when I wanted to be good at something I knew I wasn't good at. But I have to be fair to myself and admit that it was a very vague sort of envy, not altogether mean, and it ran against the grain of my character. All the same, having to hear about this person's successes in this particular field would make me extremely unhappy, and when he told me about them I treated him as though he were being naïve, etc.

Boredom — Memories of My Life

Even the pain arising from boredom and a sense of life's pointlessness is far more bearable than the boredom itself.

Revenge

Revenge is so sweet one often wishes to be insulted so as to be able to take revenge, and I don't mean just by an old enemy, but anyone, or even (especially when in a really bad mood) by a friend.

Friendship between Two Young People—Friendship

Once heroism was gone from the world, to be replaced by universal egoism, real friendship, sacrificial friendship between people who still have active interests and ambitions, became extremely improbable. So even though people have always said that equality is one of the most powerful catalysts of friendship, these days I reckon it's less likely for two young people to be friends than for a young person with someone older, someone who has strong feelings but is already disenchanted with the world and hence has ceased to expect happiness for himself. No longer gripped by urgent ambitions, the older man is more able to ally himself with someone who is still very involved and to develop a lively and useful interest in him, thus forming, always assuming the other has the spirit to reciprocate, a real and solid friendship. Such a situation seems rather more conducive to friendship than when both people are disenchanted, since if neither has ambitions or interests, there is nothing to build the friendship on; it would all be mere words and feelings and find no expression in action. Apply this observation to the case of myself and my fine and unusual friend, and to the fact of my having found no other such friend, despite having known and loved and been loved by people of great feeling and talent.

Compassion—Weakness

Notice how attractive we all find weakness in this world. If you see a boy coming toward you with an uncertain step and a helpless look about him, you're endeared and fall in love with the lad. If you see a pretty woman, looking faint and fragile, or if you happen to see any woman trying to do something but unable to because of the weakness of her sex, you feel moved and are perfectly capable of prostrating yourself before her weakness and accepting her as mistress of yourself and your strength, to the point of subjecting and sacrificing yourself entirely to the business of loving and protecting her. The cause of this effect is compassion, which I consider the one human passion and quality not tainted in any way by self-love. I say the one passion because even the heroism of sacrificing oneself for one's country, one's morality, or one's beloved, or likewise any other action however heroic or altruistic (and any affection however pure), is always the consequence of our feeling that this line of behavior offers greater satisfaction than others available in the circumstances. And every product of our minds, whatever it may be, always has its certain and inevitable origin in egoism, however chastened the egoism and however remote from it the consequent action may seem. But the compassion that springs in our hearts when we see someone suffering is a miracle of nature, a feeling totally independent of personal advantage or pleasure, entirely directed toward others and in no way mixed up with ourselves. That is why compassionate men are so rare and why pity, especially these days, is rated one of the most praiseworthy and distinguishing qualities of the sensitive, virtuous man. Unless of course the compassion turns out to be partly grounded in the fear that we might ourselves one day be subject to the same frailty we are observing. (Because self-regard is extremely subtle, it creeps in everywhere, lurking in the most hidden corners of our hearts, places you would never have thought it could penetrate.) Still, when you think it over, you'll find that spontaneous compassion does exist, entirely free of such a fear and wholly directed toward the sufferer.

Compassion toward Animals

Having sold an ox to a butcher and taken the animal to be slaughtered, at the crucial moment a peasant from the town of Recanati hesitated; he couldn't decide whether to stay or go, whether to watch or turn away, and when finally curiosity got the better of him and he saw the ox crash to the ground, he burst into tears. I heard this from someone who was there.

Paradoxes—Moral Etiquette—Serious Misfortune

When someone is suddenly given some really bad news, the intensity of his reaction doesn't increase in proportion to the seriousness or otherwise of the loss. In situations like this a person considers his misfortune total and vents all the grief he's capable of, so that even if things turned out to be twice as bad he would hardly be able to weep twice as much. I mean if at the start the news had been twice as bad, because if on the other hand he first hears of one disaster then another, this would indeed lead to greater grief, though even then the increase would hardly be in proportion to the extent of the new disaster because his mind would already be worn out and as it were numbed by the first. Yesterday, at a fair, two boys were killed by a stone falling from a roof. Word went round that the sons were brothers, children of the same mother. Afterward people were relieved when it turned out that actually they had different mothers. So here we have people cheering up in response to a grief actually doubling, since now two women will be feeling awful, while one would have felt more or less the same grief over one boy as over two. Stunned by the news, she would hardly have been able to suffer more if the catastrophe doubled. Unless of course the death of these two meant the death of all her children, which would alter the nature of the calamity and move it into a different category. It might also be true that a single child lost was an only child, in which case again these thoughts wouldn't apply.

Glory. Fame

Glory is not a passion of the absolutely primitive, solitary man, but the first time a group of men got together to kill a wild beast or do something that required their helping each other, then the most obviously courageous ones would have heard the others tell them, "Well done," frankly and without flattery, since there was no flattery in those times. The words sounded good, and so for the first time these men and any other magnanimous spirits present experienced a desire for praise. Thus the love of glory was born.

Civilization. Process of Civilization— Glory. Fame—Of Nature

So glory is a passion typical of man in society, and so natural that even now, with the world moribund as it is and in the absence of any kind of stimulus, young people still feel the need to distinguish themselves, and not finding any of the previous paths to glory open to them they burn up their energy and youth studying all the [libidinous] arts, risking their health and shortening their lives, not so much out of a craving for pleasure, but so as to be noticed and envied and to crow over conquests that are shameful but that the world applauds anyway these days, since young people just don't have any other way of taking advantage of their bodies and winning attention for what they do with them. Even the mind has only a tiny chance these days, though it may still find some paths to glory, but the body, the part of ourselves that is busiest, and that in the nature of things constitutes for most men the greater part of valor, has no other road at all.

Civilization. Process of Civilization — Glory. Fame — Physical Strength — Of Nature

A young man entering the world wants to make his mark. It's everyone's inevitable desire. But these days an ordinary young man has no other way of doing that than the one described above, the only alternative being literature, which is equally disastrous for the body. So today glory lies with activities that are bad for one's health, whereas in the past the opposite was true. As a result, generation after generation of people are growing feebler, and this consequence of our having lost those illusions that animated people in the past then becomes another reason for the disappearance of those illusions, since people just don't have the strength to sustain them, something I've spoken about elsewhere, since great illusions of the mind demand a corresponding physical strength. We know all too well the terrifying effects of the way young people live today, something that will gradually reduce the world to a hospital. But what can you do? What other employment or hope is there today for an ordinary young man? Do you suppose he can resign himself to a life of inactivity, with no prospects, and nothing to look forward to but endless monotony and unremitting boredom? In ancient times vanity was thought to be peculiar to women, since of course women share the same desire to distinguish themselves and as a rule the only way they could do that was through their beauty. Hence their *cultus sui* [cult of themselves], which, as Celso claimed, *adimi feminis non potest* [you can't take away from a woman]. These days we still think vanity is peculiar to women, but wrongly so, because it's now almost equally typical of men, since when it comes to making a mark in the world men are reduced to more or less the same condition as women, while most older men have become useless and contemptible, lifeless, pleasureless and hopeless, just as most women used to be and still tend to become, first having the whole world talking about them, then outliving their fame in old age.

Civilization. Process of Civilization —
Glory. Fame — Of Nature

We can exclude from these considerations tradesmen, farmers, craftsmen, and workers in general, since this collapse in morals and the catastrophe consequent on it is peculiar to the leisured classes.

Compassion — Weakness

Notice how our compassion and sympathy are aroused when we see someone, anyone, going through unhappiness, trouble, or pain and too weak and feeble to come out from it. It's the same when we see someone being mistreated, however mildly, and unable to deal with it.

Man's Inclinations—Hope and Fear

If you have a bitter enemy in a certain town and you see a thunderstorm over the place, do you even vaguely hope it might kill him? So why are you afraid yourself if the same storm hovers over you, when the chances of its striking are so remote you couldn't even find a reason for hoping it would dispatch your enemy, despite the fact that hope can perfectly well spring with hardly any reason at all? The same is true of a hundred other dangers; if they were opportunities for something positive you'd feel it was ridiculous to place any hope in them, yet as dangers you fear them. So it is: however easily and groundlessly hope may spring, fear does so even more readily. But this reflection seems rather useful for calming it. So fear creates more illusions than hope.

Hope and Fear

As with hope, or any other state of mind, an advantage in the future is always greater than what we have now, so ordinarily with fear a distant calamity is more terrible than anything in the present.

Hope and Fear

So the good and bad things we're expecting are usually greater than what we have in the present. The reason for both situations is the same: imagination driven by a self-regard that is taken up with hope on the one hand or fear on the other.

Consolation — Necessity — Regret

No grief arising from misfortune is comparable to one caused by some serious and irremediable damage that we feel we brought on ourselves and could have avoided; that is, to deep and sincere regret.

Reactions to Trouble — Consolation — Necessity — Regret — Handbook of Practical Philosophy

Once when Pietrino was crying because Luigi had thrown his play stick out the window, my mother said: Don't cry, don't cry, I would have thrown it out if he hadn't. And Pietrino cheered up because he would have lost his stick anyway. Another similar and equally common reaction is when we feel better and much relieved because we've persuaded ourselves that some advantage we've missed out on was not ours for the taking, or some trouble we're in not ours to avoid; consequently we struggle to convince ourselves of this, and when we can't we feel desperate, even though the trouble is the same either way. On this point, see Epictetus's *Handbook*.

Compassion — Weakness

If you see a child, a woman, an older person, laboring hopelessly at some task that their weakness prevents them from completing, you're bound to be moved to compassion and help them if you can. And if you realize you are hindering or in some way bothering someone who is powerless to prevent you and suffering as result, then you'd have to be made of stone or criminally thoughtless to find the heart to go on.

The Ancients—Moral Etiquette—
Envy—Social Machiavellianism

Diogenes Laertius [in *Lives of the Philosophers*] writes of Chilone that προσέταττε . . . ἰσχυρὸν ὄντα πρᾷον εἶναι, ὅπως οἱ πλησίον αἰδῶνται μᾶλλον ἢ φοβῶνται. [He gave instructions that people who were physically strong should be gentle in their manners, so as to inspire respect rather than fear.] Today, in a world where egoism is so widespread, this precept needs extending to all the advantages an individual may enjoy. If you are good-looking, for example, your only chance of not being hated is to cultivate an especially easygoing manner and a certain carelessness as to your person, so as to appease the vanity of those offended by this advantage of yours, or merely by your not being at a disadvantage. The same goes if you are rich, well educated, powerful, and so on. The greater the advantage you enjoy, the more friendly, self-deprecating, and almost forgetful of yourself you will have to be, since you need to massage away this cause for hatred you carry around in yourself and that others don't have, a pure provocation that makes you hateful all by itself, without your actually doing anything arrogant or unfair or whatever. This was something the ancients knew all about; indeed, they were so convinced that individual advantages provoked hatred that they supposed the gods themselves were envious, and when things went well, they took care to ward off envy, divine and human, with the result that long periods of uninterrupted prosperity made them anxious that serious disasters must follow. See Fronto, *De bello Parthico*.

Envy

I know of a woman eager to conceive who would beat a pregnant horse fiercely with a stick, saying, You pregnant and me not? Hatred and envy for the happiness of others usually occurs over things we want and haven't got, or which we'd like to be the only ones to have, or the most important, so that our name is associated with the thing. We're not generally envious of things that don't interest us, however wonderful they may be. All the same, despite the fact that envy is usually felt toward our peers, their being the only people we're ordinarily in competition with, still the intensity of this emotion can lead people to envy and hatred of others for other things.

Hatred of Our Peers — Of Nature

Hate, like love, is mostly directed toward people like ourselves; we never look for revenge on an animal with the same intensity we do on an enemy. And note: when someone has hurt us without meaning to, we still feel more resentful toward him than we would toward an animal that has hurt us deliberately and more seriously.

Compassion — Weakness

We are far more moved by a swallow that sees its young carried off and struggles helplessly to protect them than by a tiger or other wild beast in the same situation. See Virgil, Georgics 4. *Qualis populea moerens philomela sub umbra.* [Just as the nightingale, mourning in the shade of the poplar . . .], etc.

Objects of Compassion—Compassion—Weakness—
Poet—Theory of the Arts. Practical Part

Compassion often leads to love, but only when it is directed toward an object either lovable in itself or lovable when you add compassion. This is the compassion that engages us and lasts and that returns to mind again and again. However great the calamity and however innocent its victim, if that victim is not lovable, but old perhaps, or ugly, our compassion will be short-lived and usually die away when the person or the image conjured up by accounts of the event is no longer present to us. (And the mind won't dwell on such a person or go back to him.) Such accounts will anyway have to be intense and forcefully told if we are to be even briefly moved, while just a few words will be enough to have us sympathize with a pretty young girl, even one we don't know, just hearing the barest details of her troubles. So Socrates will always be more admired than pitied, and remains a very poor subject for tragedy. In the same way, the novelist who asks us to sympathize with an unfortunate character who is also ugly is making a huge mistake. Same goes for the poet and so on. In fact, whatever type of poetry it is and whatever the subject, the poet must be careful not to give us the impression that he himself is ugly, since when reading a beautiful poem we immediately imagine a beautiful poet. The contrast otherwise would be seriously disconcerting. All the more so if the poet talks about himself and his own misfortunes and unhappy loves, like Petrarch and so on.

Objects of Compassion — Compassion

The compassion I mentioned for a person who is not lovable is very like revulsion, the kind we feel when we see someone hurting an animal. It takes something really violent to provoke this emotion, since the smaller misfortunes of such a person or animal will hardly arouse much compassion, if any, in a healthy mind.

Objects of Compassion — Compassion — Weakness

With animals as with people compassion is to a large extent determined by the beauty of the sufferer. But aside from beauty, the fact that a large and important source of compassion lies in the different sex of the sufferer is all too evident, even when love has nothing to say to the matter. For example, when a misfortune however real also has an element of farce, you'll always see onlookers of the same sex laughing far more than those of the other are inclined or ready to; this is particularly the case with men, because just as men's feelings tend to be deeper, so their thoughtlessness and insensitivity is far more callous and brutal. And this will be true regardless of whether the sufferer is attractive, ugly, or plain. In fact, the small troubles of unattractive folks move us so little that very often we're inclined to laugh.

Moral Etiquette — Envy — Social Machiavellianism

Cleobulos, says Diogenes Laertius, συνεβούλευε . . . γυναικὶ (*uxori*) μὴ φιλοφρονεῖσθαι μηδὲ μάχεσθαι ἀλλοτρίων παρόντων · τὸ μὲν γὰρ ἄνοιαν, τὸ δὲ μανίαν σημαίνει [advised men not to sweettalk their wives or argue with them in the presence of strangers, since the one course betrayed stupidity and the other madness]. See p. 233.

He also advised, μὴ ἐπιγελᾶν τοῖς σκωπτομένοις · ἀπεχθήσεσ–θαι γὰρ τούτοις [against jeering at those who were an object of mockery, since if you did they would hate you].

With regard to what I said on p. 68* in the thought *Watch*, Laertius says that Chilone προσέταττε . . . λέγοντα μὴ κινεῖν τὴν χεῖρα · μανικὸν γὰρ [advised people not to wave their arms about when they talked, since he reckoned such behavior a sign of madness]. See Isaac Casaubon's note on Laertius's *Life of Polemo*, bk. 4, § 16.

> *Watch two, three or more people from behind when one of them is talking and you'll immediately understand which one is speaking; but if, standing the same distance away, you're not in a position to see, you'll never guess, unless of course you're familiar with the speaker's voice, or for other reasons. Once I had this experience of not understanding when I couldn't see, then understanding at first glance on seeing the group from behind. Because even the calmest people (and this was one of them) always move when they talk.

Moral Etiquette — Envy — Social Machiavellianism

Et si elles (les Françoises) ont un amant, elles ont autant de soin de ne pas donner à l'heureux mortel des marques de prédilection en public, qu'un Anglois du bon ton de ne pas paroître amoureux de sa femme en compagnie. [And if they (French women) have a lover, they take as much care not to give the lucky mortal any sign of their favor in public as an Englishman with good taste has not to seem to be in love with his wife when in company.] Morgan, *France*, tome 1, 1818, p. 253, bk. 3.

Happiness—Harmony of Nature—Of Nature— Handbook of Practical Philosophy

Cheerfulness, unlike worrying and resentment, very often gives rise to kindness and generosity. This is something we all know and have seen, so I won't stop to look into the reasons, which are easy enough to work out. But I will just dwell a moment on the harmony of nature which, intent as ever on the happiness of all living creatures and hence favoring cheerfulness as the most common condition in the natural order, chose to have it go hand in hand with pleasantness toward one's fellow men, the highest virtue in society, so that cheerfulness turns out to be useful not only to the cheerful individual but also to others, and serves society by having men treat each other as they should.

Courage—Paradoxes—Alarm—Ghosts (Fear of)

Alarm and terror, though more intense than fear, are often much less cowardly; in fact, sometimes they are quite free from cowardice and, unlike fear, can occur even in the most courageous men. For example, the alarm provoked by the prospect of an extremely unhappy life, or one that is long and extremely tedious. The terror of ghosts, which is childish and based on childish ideas,

was (and still is) common in very courageous people. See pp. 531*
and 535.†

     *To say nothing of the fears and alarms typical of childhood
(due to lack of experience and knowledge, coupled with a vivid
imagination that's still innocent and fresh): fear of every kind
of danger, fear of phantoms and monsters, something that happens only at that age and no other; fear of ghosts, dreams, corpses,
bumps in the night, crafted images, which are frightening at that
age but hardly bother us later, masks, for example (see my *Essay
on the Popular Errors of the Ancients*). This particular fear was so
terrible then that no calamity, or horror, no danger however dreadful, has the same power at any other age to arouse the distress, agitation, horror, shivers, in short torment, typical of those so-called
childish fears. The idea of ghosts, the spiritual, supernatural, the
holy fear of another world that often troubles us in childhood, has
something so dreadful and frantic about it that it cannot be compared to any other unhappy feeling people have later on in life.
Not even the dying man's fear of hell can be so profoundly terrible, I don't think. Because childish and primitive sensations can
penetrate and invade the innermost part and deepest root of our
minds and hearts, seizing and shaking it, but later on experience
and reason render this part of us inaccessible to any sort of feeling.

     †This can be seen in the physical or outer effects of the inner
sensations mentioned, effects regarding health, movements, gestures, or again in the decisions and actions these sensations prompt
children and primitive people to take, sweeping them along with
an overwhelming force and unstoppable violence, such as in other
ages and conditions can be prompted only by outer and physical
sensations, not by inner ones, and then only occasionally. There
it is: in childhood and in the natural state, it seems, the imagina-

tion, or the internal sensations have the same or a similar force and reality that external and mechanical sensations and forces have in other ages and conditions.

The Ancients—Civilization. The Process
of Civilization—Of Nature

We might say that in the beginning man's passions and feelings were up on the surface, then they hunkered right down in the darkest depths of the soul, and finally they came up to a midpoint where they have stayed put. Because natural man, extremely sensitive though he may be, wears his passions on the surface, venting them in all the many external manifestations suggested and designed by nature to clear a way for this irresistible rush and impetus of feeling, which, precisely because so violent in its manifestation and so immediately expressed, soon abates after this grand outward surging, though it does occur rather frequently. A man no longer in the natural state, but still with something of nature about him, feels the same intensity of passion as the primitive man, or almost, but bottles it all up inside and shows no trace of it, or only fleeting, ambiguous hints; his feelings hunker down in the depths, where they grow stronger and more resilient, and if they are painful feelings, denied the outlet nature demands, they become a torment which will be of greater or lesser intensity according to the quality of the individual and the emotion; in some cases they may even kill. There are still people like this around today, because, aside from some of the common crowd, no one is so close to the natural state as to allow his passions to surge up to the surface (except in some extreme cases where nature triumphs): but many people are sufficiently close to nature to feel passion with intensity and keep it hidden, locked away in the depths of their minds. These people definitely belong to a middle era, between the natural state and the present, when real feeling was neither so ordinarily talked about nor so rarely experienced as it is today. The perfectly modern man almost never experiences passions or feelings that rush to outward expression or dig down inside; rather, all his passions are held, so to speak, at the midpoint of his mind, by which I mean that he is not moved by them, or only mildly, and hence is left free to exercise all his natural faculties, habits, and so on. With the result that he passes most of his life in an emotionless state and hence grows bored, experiencing no strong or really powerful sensations. Example. A friend or someone you're eager to see returns after a long absence or you meet him for the first time. A child or savage will hug this person, touch him, dance about and give a thousand outward signs of the sincere joy he intensely feels; there's nothing fake about these manifestations, they're very real and very natural. The man of feeling, making no extravagant gestures or movements, will shake his hand, or at most embrace him slowly, and stay a while in this embrace, or some other position, giving no sign of the joy he feels other than his stillness and the steadiness of his gaze, and maybe a tear or two, and although inside his state of mind has completely changed, outside he remains more or less as before. Ordinary man, or the man whose feelings have been dulled and diminished by his dealings with the world and his depressing knowledge of how things are, in short modern man, will remain as he always was, inside and out, won't feel emotion, or not much, less than he expected to, even, and whether or not he foresaw it, for him the event will be just another ordinary moment in his life, one of those pleasures we experience without emotion and that, however eagerly looked forward to, are no sooner with us than they seem cold and ordinary and quite incapable of moving us or filling our lives.*

*What I said on pp. 266–268 will serve as a rule for playwrights portraying characters in different periods.

Compassion — Weakness

That nightingale Virgil talks about in the Orpheus episode, huddled on a branch all night long, lamenting the loss of its stolen young and expressing through its *pitiful song* a profound, constant, and extremely poignant grief without looking for revenge or compensation for its suffering and without trying to recover what's been lost, etc. arouses intense compassion, because of the helplessness it expresses.

Hope — Suicide

Men never lose hope in response to nature but rather in response to reason. So people (the authors of the *Morale universelle*, vol. 3) who say no one can kill himself without first sinking into madness, since in your right mind you never lose hope, have it all wrong. Actually, leaving religious belief out of the equation, our going on hoping and living is a happy, natural, but also real and constant madness, and something quite contrary to reason which all too clearly shows that there is no hope for any of us.

The French — Hope

Nisi quod magnae indolis signum est, sperare semper. [All the same it is the mark of great character to go on hoping always.] Florus IV, 8.

Hope — Memories of My Life

Hope, I mean a spark of it, a crumb, never deserts us, not even after we suffer the kind of calamity that is diametrically opposed to hoping and absolutely decisive.

No One to Do You a Favor — Illusions — Of Nature

I talked elsewhere* about asking someone a favor he refuses to do for you because it would bring on him the hatred of someone else, etc. The reason for this is that hatred is passion, gratitude is reason and duty, unless of course the favor produces the passion of love, since there's no doubt that love is often more effective and active than hatred and the other passions. But mere gratitude is entirely directed toward someone else, while passionate love, for all it might seem to be so, is not, but is grounded first and foremost in our self-regard, in that we love this person as someone who arouses our interest, who gives us pleasure, and our person is thus very much involved in this affection. But reason is never as effective as passion. Read the philosophers: we have to arrange things, they say, so that man acts on reason as much as, or rather far more than, on passion, or rather no, purely out of reason and duty. Baloney. Man's nature and the world's can certainly be corrupted, but not corrected. And if we let nature have its way, things would be fine, despite this dominance of passion over reason. The thing is not to stifle passion with reason but to transform reason into passion; have duty, virtue, heroism, and so on become passions. And so of their natures they are. So they were for people in ancient times, and things were the better for it. But when the only passion in the world is our egoism, then people are perfectly right to rail against passion. But how can we stifle egoism with reason if reason actually feeds egoism by breaking down our illusions? And even if egoism were stifled, a man who has no passions would not act on his illusions, or on his reason either, because that's how things are, and they can't be changed: reason is not a living, driving force, and man is just going to get more and more shiftless, idle, static, apathetic, and sluggardly, something he has already very largely become.

*If you ask someone a favor he can't do without having someone else hate him for it, it's extremely unlikely (other things being equal) that he'll do it for you even though you're the best of friends. Of course, in provoking another's hatred he would have strengthened the friendship with you, perhaps enormously, so it might seem that the gains and losses even out. But the truth is that hate counts more than love, since hatred is by far the more active of the two. Modern psychologists would leave it at that without bothering to look for the principle behind this imbalance, which actually is all too obvious, our self-regard. Because a person acting on his hatred acts for himself while one acting out of love does so for another; a man taking revenge furthers his own interests, a man doing good is thinking of someone else, and no one is ever so passionately generous as to do more for others than he does for himself.

Patience—Resignation—Handbook of Practical Philosophy

Une résistance inutile (aux malheurs) retarde l'habitude qu'elle (l'âme) contracteroit avec son état. Il faut céder aux malheurs. Renvoyez-les à la patience: c'est à elle seule à les adoucir. [Pointless resistance (to misfortunes) only delays the moment when it (the soul) will be inured to the situation. Better yield to adversity. Respond with patience: only patience can soften calamity.] Mme de Lambert, *Avis d'une mère à son fils.* In Paris and Lyon 1808, p. 88.

Arrogance

Demetrius of Phalerum τῶν τετυφωμένων ἀνδρῶν ἔφη τὸ μὲν ὕψος δεῖν περιαιρεῖν, τὸ δὲ φρόνημα καταλιπεῖν. (Laertius, in *Demetrius*, bk. 5, § 82). Which in Latin is: *hominum fastu turgidorum aiebat circumcidi oportere altitudinem, opinionem autem de se relinquere.* [He said that arrogant men should be stripped of their haughtiness and left with their pride.] An excellent translation. But Méric Casaubon in his idiotic comment on a few words a little later in the same section gives Τοὺς φίλους ἐπὶ μὲν τὰ ἀγαθὰ παρακαλουμένους ἀπιέναι, ἐπὶ δὲ τὰς συμφορὰς, αὐτομάτους. [He said that friends turn up to happy occasions only if invited but come running of their own accord to a calamity.] What was meant was, "they should come running," taking δεῖν, "they should," from the previous sentence. Attributed again to Demetrius, in Laertius, loc. cit., § 83.

Illusions — Of Nature

Nature can and does make up for reason's shortcomings on endless occasions, but reason can never make up for what is lacking in nature, not even when it seems to produce great actions: this happens rarely enough, and even then the driving, motive force doesn't actually come from reason but from nature. Conversely, take away nature's drive and reason is always left idle and impotent.

Satirical Thoughts — Courage — Hope — Hope and Fear — Fear

People who think every minor illness they have is serious, or worse than it actually is, tend, when they have a serious, perhaps fatal, illness, to think it minor or less serious than it is. The reason for both tendencies is cowardice, which prompts them to fear when there's nothing to fear and to hope when there's no hope to be had.

Impatience — Intense Willfulness — Handbook of Practical Philosophy — Memories of My Life

There's nothing perhaps that spurs us to action and makes us impatient to achieve our goal so much as our not being sure of achieving it, though this is true only when the goal is important for us and the idea of our not achieving it depressing. This is not just because our being unsure forces us to take action (while being sure of ourselves we might get lazy), on the grounds that a goal we can't be certain of achieving requires a greater effort. But even when our task doesn't require a greater effort, which might well be the case (just as there are goals one can be certain of achieving on condition of making a considerable effort), and quite regardless of the actual usefulness of our efforts or whether they're necessary or not, we'll still be extremely industrious and terribly impatient to achieve our goal, simply because we can't bear the uncertainty and so yearn to be free from the constant worry caused by our not being sure of achieving this thing we've set our hearts on. Perhaps we'd prefer to be certain of failing than to be in this constant state of worry. Even when it comes to physical things, I've often found myself doubting whether I was strong enough to finish something I really cared about, and hence redoubled my efforts impatiently, even when friends advised me to ease off because there was no harm in taking more time over the job. But I couldn't deal with being unsure about something that was so important to me, whereas if I'd been sure of finishing I'd have had no trouble taking more time over it. To the point that my very impatience was in danger of jeopardizing the outcome, by depriving me of the necessary rest, and so on. Same thing with writing, and so on. Same if you have to complete a job in a given time and you're worried you won't make it, your impatience and work rate don't increase in relation to any need, they go beyond that, with the result that, if possible, you end up finishing the job before your deadline.*

*But note that very often this impatience risks compromising the outcome. Eager to see things finished anyhow, to put the fear that we won't achieve our goal behind us, we don't do things as well as we could have if we hadn't been anxious and had gone about the job more calmly, with less fuss, and so on, in short if we'd been willing to hang on and allow things to proceed as they ought to have, in the proper amount of time, etc. In short, very often in some matter we're not sure of, albeit not of the greatest importance, by hurrying to be done, not so much out of a yearning to achieve our goal but because impatient with our own doubting, we fail to do what we wanted: and this happens in our trivial, daily, practical chores as well. Watch those words *not so much out of a yearning*, etc., which is where this thought has something new and to the point about it; everybody knows about the effects of impatience, but they attribute those effects to an impatience *to achieve*.

Ancients — Christianity — Moral Etiquette — Envy

The idea the ancients had of man's happiness (and hence unhappiness) in this life, his glory and achievements, and how all this seemed real and solid to them, can also deduced from this: that they believed the gods themselves were envious of great human happiness and great human achievements, and hence they feared this divine envy and took care to ward it off, to the point that they even thought themselves lucky when they suffered a small setback and (if I remember rightly) would actually inflict such setbacks on themselves to satisfy the Gods and appease their envy. *Deos immortales precatus est, ut, si quis eorum invideret OPERIBUS ac fortunae suae, in ipsum potius saevirent, quam in remp.* [He prayed the immortal gods, asking that if any of them envied his *achievements* and his good fortune they should strike him, not the state.] Velleius, bk. 1, ch. 10, on Aemilius Paullus. And so it was: two of his sons died, one four days before his triumph and the other three days afterward. See the *Variorum* notes. Also Dionysius of Halicarnassus, bk. 12, chs. 20 and 23, Milan ed., and Mai's note on ch. 20.3. That is, the ancients considered human affairs so important that they assumed the gods' desires and goals were the same as ours; they saw the gods as involved in our lives and our wealth and hence supposed them jealous of our happiness and achievements, as if they were our peers, never doubting that men were worthy of the envy of the immortals.*

> *Hic* sive invidia deum, *sive fato, rapidissimus procurrentis imperii cursus parumper Gallorum Senonum incursione subprimitur.* [At this point, whether *out of divine envy* or fate's will, the empire's extremely rapid advance was briefly halted by the invasion of the Senonian Gauls.] Florus, 1, 13, beginning, as he starts the history of the first Gallic War.

Man's Inclinations—Hope and Fear

That fear plays a greater part in our lives than hope is also evident from this: that hope itself generates fear, so much so that even the strongest people, the least inclined to fear, are made fearful by hope, especially when they hope for something important. In fact a man is almost unable to hope without fear, and this is especially true in the case of a hope that really matters. If you hope, you also fear, while when you have no hope you have nothing to be afraid of. But looked at the other way round, hope is not generated by fear, although a person who is afraid does always hope that the thing he's afraid of won't actually happen. Note that the emotion directly opposed to fear is hope. Yet hope can't exist without producing its opposite.

Regret—Resignation

You can sleep on any sorrow resulting from whatever trouble, but there's no sleeping on regret. There is no resting and no peace with regret, which is why it's the greatest or the most bitter of all sorrows, as I have said elsewhere.

Regret

Quippe ita se res habet, ut plerumque, qui fortunam mutaturus Deus (Voss. leg. cui fortunam. al. delent τὸ *qui, et melius) consilia corrumpat, efficiatq., QUOD MISERRIMUM EST, ut quod accidit, etiam merito accidisse videatur, et casus in culpam transeat.* [That's how these things usually go: when a God decides to destroy a successful man (Voss. has *cui fortunam*; others omit τὸ *qui*, which reads better), he deranges his mind, so that—and this is the worst of it—everything that goes wrong seems no more than what he deserved, and hence bad luck morphs into guilt.] Velleius, 2, 118, § 4.

Communicating Pleasures to Others—Moral Handbook

Della Casa writes (*Galateo*, ch. 3) that "when as sometimes happens someone sees something disgusting by the roadside, it is hardly polite to turn to one's friends and point it out to them, and even less so to hold out something that stinks for someone else to smell, as some people do, making quite a fuss and even sticking it under your nose, and saying: Come on, check out the smell of this." So it seems it's almost a natural inclination to want others to share not only in our pleasures but also in certain irritations (as well as the sorrows coming from our troubles), and we enjoy their sharing these emotions and it bothers us if we can't have them do that. You'll infer from this that man is made to live in society, but I think, on the contrary, that although this inclination, or desire, may seem natural, it's actually a response to living in society, though one that kicks in quickly and easily, because you find it in children as well as adults, and perhaps more often in children than adults. See p. 208* and p. 85,† end.

> *Not only beauty, but perhaps most of the facts and truths that we believe to be absolute and general, are relative and particular. We get used to things and habit becomes a second nature; it happens almost without our noticing, producing and destroying endless qualities that, once acquired or lost, we soon persuade ourselves we can't have, or can't not have, ascribing to eternal and immutable laws, or to the natural system, or to Providence, etc., what is actually the result of chance and circumstances that are accidental and arbitrary. Add opinions, climates, physical and spiritual temperaments to what you acquire through habit and you'll see that few, really very few truths are absolute and inherent in the system of things. This aside from any independence from these truths to be found in other systems of things.
>
> †When our feelings of enthusiasm or whatever are not very deep, we try to find a friend we can share them with and we enjoy being able to discuss them while we're feeling them (in line with Maromontel's observation that when we see a beautiful landscape we can't be happy unless we have someone we can say *la belle campagne!* to) because in a way we hope to increase the pleasure of the feeling and the feeling itself by bringing in our friends' feelings. But when a feeling is deep, exactly the opposite happens, be-

cause we fear, and rightly, that if we share it, bringing it out from the depths of our souls and exposing it to the air of conversation, that it will lose its intensity and fade away. Aside from the fact that this feeling fills our minds and occupies our attention entirely, leaving us no space for thinking of others, nor any way of expressing our feeling to them, since that would require a certain amount of attention, which would be distracting, and distraction at this point is not just unwelcome, it's impossible.

Communicating Pleasures to Others — Secrets

People's inclination to have others share their pains and pleasures, something I've spoken about elsewhere, is largely responsible for the craving (attributed mainly to women and typical above all of children, in short the most natural, lightweight people) to reveal things or secrets that you ought, and often would actually like, to keep hidden, or to tell a piece of news immediately, some discovery, a pleasure, pain, fear, or irritation you just felt, etc., and again for all the talk involved in telling or recounting what you're thinking this minute, or what you just thought, etc., the way children can't stop themselves chattering about anything and everything.

Communicating Pleasures to Others

The desire to share one's feelings (pleasant or unpleasant as I have said elsewhere) will be more frequent and stronger the nearer a person is to nature. Children can't resist it at all, and won't ease up until by force of love, imprecation, and sheer insistence they've told whoever's around or whoever they've sought out, all their plea-

sures and pains, anything striking, any unusual sensation they've
felt or are feeling, music they've heard, good or bad, any kind of
singing or instrument that has excited them: any object they've
seen that has impressed them, etc., whether for better or worse. In
similar circumstances the coarsest, most ignorant and uneducated
folk, common people in general, can't help shouting to anyone in
the vicinity, *look look, listen listen.* And this exclamation is so natural that even in a big crowd of people at the same event, all or lots
of them will shout it out just the same, without anyone in particular listening to them and without their taking care to be heard by
anyone in particular. But no one can stop himself shouting out this
way, thus making plain this natural inclination that has us wanting,
craving to share things with others. And note that people who have
a strong feeling when they're on their own often come out with this
same exclamation without anyone's being around to hear them:
and we say, *look* and *listen* when there's no one around to look or
listen, and hence we try any way we can to procure the illusion of
having satisfied a desire that can't in reality be satisfied. And though
this happens more often the more primitive a person is, and the
more susceptible he is to marveling at things or feeling *strong* and
lively sensations; nevertheless it is extremely frequent in the best-
educated of men, etc., and if you watch out you'll see how often
we do it ourselves every day without realizing. We do it, I mean,
either alone, talking to ourselves, or in company. And there is no
one, I'm sure, however taciturn and loath to speaking, conversing,
and *communicating with others* he may be, who, on experiencing a
really strong and lively feeling, doesn't feel obliged, almost in spite
of himself, or without having time to think, and without realizing it

even, to come out with suchlike exclamations that demonstrate his desire and intention to communicate what he feels to others and share it with them.

Self-Regard — Compassion

Aside from compassion there is one other natural emotion that is quite free from self-regard, and which though it resembles compassion is not the same thing. This is that very distinct, acute distress we feel when we see, for example, a child doing something we know will cause him harm: or a man exposing himself to some evident danger; or a person close to going over the edge of a precipice, without realizing it. And suchlike. Disasters about to happen. Then we feel we absolutely must intervene, if we can, and if we can't our pain intensifies. Certainly, seeing someone doing himself harm, or about to suffer, whether voluntarily or unawares, etc., seeing and not intervening, or not feeling distress at not being able to intervene, is unnatural. Equally, when harm is actually done, seeing someone fall, etc., even if the harm is not of the kind that looks horrible and sickening, nevertheless we naturally and *without meaning to* feel seriously distressed. Observed carefully, these emotive impulses are distinct from compassion, which comes after harm is done, not before or simultaneous with it. Same is true for inanimate things, or creatures of other species: when we see a beautiful, precious, rare, useful object, or what do I know, an animal, etc., destroyed, or in danger of being destroyed or damaged, we feel the same painful emotion, the same need to yell out, to intervene if we can, etc. And this even when the thing doesn't belong to anyone in particular and its being damaged or destroyed will harm no one in particular. Hence the distress we feel at moments like this is felt directly for the object about to be damaged, and perhaps the same is true when the object does have an owner and that owner is someone we care for. They say a woman is really strong when she can see a piece of her crockery broken without getting upset. But not just women; men too; and not just our own things, but other people's, or things owned in common, or ownerless, just so long as they have a certain value, seeing them about to be damaged we have the same feelings, whether we want to or not. The root of this feeling does not seem to be located in self-regard. It seems our nature has a certain interest in anything that's worth something, a certain horror at seeing such a thing destroyed, even when it has nothing to do with us. See the following page.* The horror of destruction (which might in the last analysis be traced back to self-regard) does not seem to play any part in this, or not an important part. All day long we see thousands of unimportant things being destroyed without feeling bad or making any attempt to prevent it.

*It seems that nature has charged us all, jointly, to provide for the preservation of *everything good* (note these words which could hugely extend the scope of this thought, for example to morality, to beauty of every kind, material and immaterial, etc.) and to protect it from destruction, something that would cause real damage to each of us in his degree. In this sense perhaps one could in the long run refer this emotion to self-regard, or maybe not.

Ancients — Childhood — Memories of My Life

As with pleasures, pains are much more intense for primitive man and in childhood than in our own age and condition, and for the same reasons that their pleasures are more intense. First (especially with children) these people haven't had time to grow inured to good and bad. So good and bad are felt more strongly and act more forcibly on their minds than on ours. Then (and this is the main point, and something common to all men in the natural state) pain, distress, whatever, for a child or primitive person, suddenly and unexpectedly replaces the perception of a possible or even achieved happiness; so it comes in sharpest possible contrast to an impression of well-being that he imagines is real and considerable, a well-being he has either already experienced or is hoping for with a steadfast hope, or presently seeing in others; instead distress is the opposite, depriving him of a happiness he believes is real, solid, absolutely achievable, man's destiny indeed, something others already have, and that he could have, if only this obstacle hadn't gotten in his way, whether for now, or forever. Likewise the idea of absolute evil, independently, I mean, of any comparison with the good, is perhaps stronger in the natural state than in a state of knowledge and civilization.

Remember that intense gloom we felt as children, when some game or holiday was over. It is only natural that such pain should correspond to our previous expectations, to the joy that came before it. And that the pain of disappointment should be in proportion to the hope we'd entertained. I'm not saying in proportion to any pleasure we really felt, since even children are never *satisfied* by their pleasure, given that, as I've said elsewhere, no living being could ever be satisfied unless by a pleasure that was infinite. Rather our gloom, after games or holidays, was inconsolable not so much because the pleasure was over as because it hadn't matched up to our hopes. So that sometimes we experienced a kind of remorse or regret, as if it was our own fault we hadn't enjoyed things properly. Because experience hadn't yet taught us to hope for little, prepare ourselves for disappointment, and get used to making do with such or even greater frustrations, etc.

In short, we took things seriously at that age, or more seriously than at other times of life (both relatively and in particular, and generally and absolutely), so it was only natural that both our pleasures and pains were greater, in proportion to how much more seriously we took the objects of pain and pleasure.

So when we were hoping for something, how worried we'd be, how anxious and nervous, hearts trembling at every small hitch, every apparent difficulty that might prevent us from getting what we were hoping for!

And then if we didn't get what we were hoping for (however small that thing may seem to our eyes today), how desperate we'd be! To the point that later perhaps, faced with life's great disasters, we never felt, nor ever will feel such pain and heartbreak as we did for those trivial childish setbacks.

Friendship—Communicating Pleasures to Others— Handbook of Practical Philosophy—Memories of My Life

Quid dulcius, quam habere, quicum omnia audeas sic loqui,

ut tecum? Quis esset tantus fructus in prosperis rebus, nisi haberes, qui illis aeque, ac tu ipse, gauderet? [What is sweeter than to have someone you feel you can say everything to, as you would to yourself? And what pleasure would there be in the good times if you didn't have someone to share all your joy?] Cicero, *Laelius sive de amicitia*, ch. 6.

Pleasure of Dwelling on Things

Les habitants du Midi craignant beaucoup la mort, l'on s'étonne d'y trouver des institutions qui la rappellent à ce point; mais il est dans la nature d'aimer à se livrer à l'idée même que l'on redoute. Il y a comme un enivrement de tristesse qui fait à l'âme le bien de la remplir tout entière. [Fearing death as much as they do, one is surprised to find that the people of the South have institutions that remind them of it so intensely; but it is natural to give ourselves up to thoughts of the things we fear. There is a sort of intoxicating sadness that fills the soul to the brim and does it good.] *Corinne*, bk. 10, ch. 1, tome 2, p. 115, edition cited above. In this regard one might note that vague but real impulse we feel when, for example, we have something that stinks in our hands to have a quick smell of it. Likewise if you happen to pass by, let's say, some place where they're executing someone, you're revolted at the thought, but I'm ready to bet you'll find you can't not sneak a quick look, then turn away at once. In this regard see an interesting moment in Plato, *Opera*, ed. Ast, tome 4, p. 236, ll. 8–16. It's the same with everything that turns our stomachs; so if you've survived a serious danger, something frightening, thinking about it stops your heart, you don't have the strength to dwell on that moment, that thing that happened, how close you were to death, etc., but nor do you have the strength to get rid of the thought, so that inevitably between the wanting and the not wanting you end up having as it were a quick look. It's the same if some thought pops up that saddens you, some memory that makes you feel ashamed of yourself. The reason this time is definitely not the intoxication Staël talks about, nor curiosity, as anyone who thinks about it will see. Rather it seems that the unknown irks us more than the known, and since this thing frightens us, or gives us the shivers or saddens us, we can't leave it be, and despite our revulsion we feel the urge to give it a good long look and get to know it. Perhaps it also has to do with our love of the extraordinary and our natural hatred of monotony and boredom, something innate in us all, so that when we are presented with something that breaks the monotony, and takes us out of the ordinary, even if it's something seriously worse than our boredom that perhaps for the moment we're hardly aware of and not thinking about at all, all the same the shock and upset we get from a quick look at this revolting thing gives us a certain pleasure. This explanation moves us closer to Staël, since boredom is nothing other than the emptiness of the soul, which is then filled, as she says, by this thought and for a moment entirely taken up with it. Finally the phenomenon may also derive, and I think at least in part it does, from the very fear we have of the thought, for the same reason that, in all things physical and moral, our wanting something too intensely and fearing we won't get it distracts us from our end, our beginning some manual task, a surgical operation for example, too determinedly while afraid of making mistakes, compromises the outcome, and in literature or the fine arts, our trying too hard for simplicity, and fearing we won't achieve it, in fact leads to our not achieving it, etc.

Communicating Pleasure to Others

With regard to our natural inclination to share any unusual emotions, pleasant or unpleasant, with others, see a famous moment in Cicero (*Laelius, sive de amicitia,* all of ch. 23). I think this passage is the first mention of this phenomenon which is so well known and familiar to us in modern times.

Charity—Desperation—Resignation—Handbook of Practical Philosophy—Memories of My Life

We all know that a man who's been through the worst, who's disappointed with life and has given up any hope of happiness, though he's still not been brought to the desperation only death can lay to rest, is naturally and effortlessly inclined to serve others and be charitable, even toward people he doesn't care about at all, and maybe even finds hateful. This is not the energy of heroism, since a man in this state is not capable of any energy of spirit at all; it's rather as if, having no interest or hope in yourself, you switched your interest and hope to other people's lives and hence aimed to fill your mind, keep it occupied and revive these two emotions we just mentioned, interest in something, which means having some purpose to aim at, and hope, without which life is not life or doesn't recognize itself as such and has no sense of itself. The fact is that when a man finds himself in this position, I mean desperate, not in such a way as to hate himself (which is desperation in its ferocious crisis) but so as not to be looking out for himself, not to be thinking of his own well-being; not only does he take pleasure in serving others, but he develops a certain affection for their lives (even when, as I said, they're people he hardly knows), feels a certain commitment, an engagement, etc., albeit quite listlessly, since he's not capable of strong, lively emotions, but all the same a far keener interest in other people's welfare than he's ever felt before. And this happens absolutely as soon as a man is reduced to this condition, as though a sudden change had come over him: it even happens to men who've been steeped in selfishness. In short, thoughts of other people's lives fill his mind almost entirely replacing thoughts of his own, which disappears, forgotten, given up for lost, no longer capable of hope or happiness, without which life lacks purpose and direction. And his desire, interest, hope for happiness, that can no longer be channeled toward his own happiness—something impossible, even to attempt it would be to waste those energies that the mind needs for sustenance—are directed to other people's happiness: and this spontaneously, without a trace of heroism. So the spirit of the man who has lost any hope of happiness and hence is morally dead, is resurrected into a listless afterlife; nevertheless, resurrected he is and alive in others, or rather in the purpose of achieving happiness for others, which has become his purpose. Like those bodies with corrupt, unhealthy blood, incapable of life, that some doctors emptied (or proposed emptying) of their own blood, to bring them back to a measure of health by filling them with another person's blood, or an animal's; almost changing the person and transforming someone who was no longer capable of life into someone who was: keeping alive a person no longer able to live for himself.

Another cause of this behavior is as follows: our man, though desperate, does not hate himself (a situation that usually occurs not, as you might suppose, before someone starts to hate himself, but after he has hated himself intensely and to no end, with the result that having looked for satisfaction every way it can, his self-regard is entirely crushed and his mind, now exhausted by its efforts, is reduced to the calm and quiet of a lassitude entirely incapable of any intense emotion), this man, without hating himself, as I said, but simply thinking of himself and his own life as pointless, gets some gratification and satisfaction, some (but very little) consolation, in finding situations where he can make himself and his life useful, since otherwise it would be of no use at all; and this making any use whatsoever of a self and life already tossed aside as absolutely useless, while it may not bring him any benefit at all and though he is no longer capable of entertaining any illusions or of imagining he might achieve great things, nevertheless comforts him and allows him to think of himself as a little less useless; or if nothing else (and rather) as having at least used, and not tossed away, these leftovers of existence and living, and physical strength.

Charity—Desperation—Resignation—Handbook of Practical Philosophy—Memories of My Life

Finding themselves excluded from life, they try to live somehow in others, not out of love for them, and hardly even for love of themselves, but because despite having lost their own lives, they still have an existence to fill and to feel any way they can.

The Ancients—Charity—Civilization. Process of
Civilization—Desperation—Resignation—Handbook
of Practical Philosophy—Memories of My Life

Nature's desperation is always ferocious, frenetic, bloody; it
doesn't yield to necessity or fortune but looks to overcome them
in itself, through injury to itself, through its own death, etc. That
docile, quiet, resigned desperation that today someone who has lost
all hope of happiness, because of the human condition in general
or his own circumstances in particular, tends to yield to, coming
to terms with life and putting up with the passing time and years,
bowing to what he sees as unavoidable; this desperation, though
it originally derived from the natural kind, in ways I've explained
above, actually has more to do with reason and philosophy, and
hence is peculiar to and typical of modern times. In fact, these days
one might say that anyone who has a certain level of intelligence
and feeling, having had some experience of the world, and in particular people like this who've reached maturity and haven't been
fortunate in life, will fall into this state of quiet desperation and stay
in it till they die. It's a state that was almost totally unknown to the
ancients and likewise to young people today when they are sensitive, generous, and unfortunate. The first kind of desperation causes
hatred of self (because the sufferer still has enough self-regard to be
capable of hating himself), but concern and respect for things. The
second kind causes neglect, contempt, and coldness toward things
and a kind of languid love of oneself (since the sufferer doesn't have
enough self-regard to summon the energy to hate himself) that resembles neglect, but love it is, though not such as to lead a person

to worry very much, or grieve, or pity his own bad luck, and even less to struggle, or try to do anything for himself, cool as he is toward everything and having almost lost the feel and sense of his spirit, and grown a thick skin over his faculty for feeling and desiring, for passions and affection and so on, and having likewise almost lost, from long habit and long and relentless attrition, almost all the elasticity of the soul's springs and resources. Ordinarily, people like this are mostly concerned with keeping things as they are, plodding along with their methodical lives, changing nothing, doing nothing new, not because they are fearful or idle—before they fell into this state they'll have been quite the opposite—but out of a reluctance that comes from their experience of adversity and prompts them to fear that any new development would upset this restfulness, quietness, slumber, into which after long struggles and much resistance their spirits have finally fallen, withdrawn, huddled up in themselves almost. The world today is full of people living in this second kind of desperation (while among the ancients the first sort was extremely common). It's not hard then to see just how much the enterprise, variety, mobility, and vitality of this world will stand to gain when all the best minds, I think we can say, on reaching maturity, become incapable of action, and of no use to themselves or to others.

Children—Sorrow—Memories of My Life

No one perhaps is so unimportant to us that we are not moved when he says his farewells setting off for this or that destination, or takes leave of us on whatever occasion, and tells us, *We will never meet again*; however cool we are to him, those words are bound to make us feel more or less sad. The horror and fear man has, on the one hand of nothingness and on the other of *eternity*, turn up everywhere, and *never again* can't be heard without a shiver. Natural effects are to be sought in natural persons who are not yet spoiled, or at least not much, or as little as possible. Today, with a very few exceptions, only children offer the chance to explore, observe, and analyze qualities, inclinations, and emotions that are truly natural. So, when I was a child this was how I behaved. When I saw someone leaving, no matter how little I cared about that person, I would try to work out whether it was possible or likely I'd see him again. If I thought I wouldn't, I'd hang around, to watch and listen to him and so on, and follow him all eyes and ears as much as I could, saying over and over to myself, till the words had sunk in deep and the thought was well settled in my head: *So this is the last time, I won't see him ever again, or, perhaps never again.* And again when someone I knew died, even if it was someone I'd never been interested in, I'd feel quite sad, not so much for him, or because I was interested in him now he was dead, but because deep down I'd be thinking over and over: *He's gone forever—forever? yes: it's all over with him: I'll never see him again: and nothing of his will ever play any part in my life.* Then if I could, I'd start going over the last time I'd seen him or listened to him, etc., and I was sad I hadn't realized it was the last time and that I hadn't behaved accordingly.

Curiosity—Science and Ignorance

La curiosité est une connoissance commencée, qui vous fait aller plus loin et plus vite dans le chemin de la vérité. [Curiosity is knowledge beginning; it will take you farther and faster along the path of truth.] Mme de Lambert, work quoted above, p. 72. I don't entirely understand what the marquise means, but here are the facts. Curiosity, or the desire to know, is for the most part nothing other than a consequence of knowledge. Consider nature and you'll see that primitive man has very little curiosity, and what he has is slight and weak; you'll see that it never enters his head to want to know about things that have nothing to do with him or that nature has hidden from him (e.g., the things of physics, astronomy, etc., the origins and destiny of man, animals, plants, the world); you'll see how incapable he is of undertaking any serious project to find out about anything, let alone anything difficult to grasp (that is, precisely the things man wasn't supposed to know about, an ignorance that kept people happy, even when they knew about other easier, more obvious things). If anything, primitive man's imagination stands in for knowledge, so that he thinks he knows the reason for something, when in fact it's not the reason, etc. In short it's just not true that man is irresistibly drawn toward truth and knowledge. Curiosity, as it is today and has been for a long time, is one of those corrupt qualities whose development and progress is quite anomalous; the same is true of many other qualities and passions; they are good and useful, necessary even, at the levels nature meant for them, but extremely negative and deadly when developed to higher levels they were never meant to reach and transformed in all kinds of ways. So that while these qualities and passions may be natural and human in their roots, they are not natural in their present form today, nor can we learn anything about nature and man's makeup from their present state, nor deduce such consequences for our future as people have deduced.*

> *In fact, natural curiosity prompts man, children, etc., to want to see, hear, etc., things that are beautiful, or extraordinary, or remarkable for the person in question. But it doesn't stimulate or torment him to know the cause of the effects he's enjoyed seeing, hearing, etc. On the contrary, in the ordinary way natural man does not go beyond marveling at things, he enjoys the pleasure that wonderment produces and is content. So primitive curiosity does not naturally prompt man to know or want to know anything beyond what is easily known (and natural man wants to know these things only so far as they are easy), things that nature hasn't hidden from us and hence knowledge of which doesn't undermine the primitive order, doesn't spoil man, doesn't run against the grain of his nature or prejudice, his happiness and perfection: since these objects of his curiosity are not part of that order of things nature wanted to keep hidden and unknown. One sees this in other animals too.

Illusions—Italian Literature—Italian Language

Les femmes apprennent volontiers l'Italien, qui me paroît dangereux, c'est la langue de l'Amour. Les Auteurs Italiens sont peu châtiés; il règne dans leurs ouvrages un jeu de mots, une imagination sans règle, qui s'oppose à la justesse de l'esprit. [Women gladly learn Italian, something I think is dangerous, it is the language of Love. Italian authors are undisciplined; their works are full of wordplay and their imagination follows no rules, it undermines sound judgment.] Mme de Lambert, work cited above, pp. 73–74.

Perfectability—Human Qualities

Examinez votre caractère, et mettez à profit vos défauts; il n'y en a point qui ne tienne à quelques vertus, et qui ne les favorise. La Morale n'a pas pour objet de détruire la nature, mais de la perfectionner. [Examine your character and turn your faults to your advantage; there's not one that doesn't possess some virtue, or that doesn't favor virtue. The purpose of morality is not to destroy nature but to perfect it.] Mme de Lambert, *Avis d'une mère à sa fille*, place quoted above, p. 84. And she goes on showing with example after example how each imperfection leads to, encourages, and almost contains a virtue, concluding: *Il n'ya pas une foiblesse, dont, si vous voulez, la vertu ne puisse faire quelque usage.* [There is no defect, which, if you so desire, virtue cannot turn to some use], place quoted above. These observations, by no means exclusive to Mme de Lambert, allow us to arrive at a very general and important truth: that those human qualities thought vicious and reckoned to be natural and innate vices actually require only the smallest modifications to be transformed and returned to good and positive qualities; that in the beginning, as originally constituted, those human qualities that now seem essentially and primordially bad were in fact good; that once those first natural qualities had been easily corrupted and diverted from their purpose, we no longer knew what positive ends they were supposed to serve and began to think of our depravity as a natural and innate vice, when actually it was something man himself had produced, and we started to confuse the improper use of qualities we call natural, with the proper use that nature meant them to have but that we can no longer easily discern.

In short, all this confirms the doctrine of man's natural and primitive perfection, since even those qualities that people think of on the one hand as natural and innate to man (and they are) and on the other as naturally bad (which they aren't) were originally good: and this mistake has people imagining that nature is vicious and in need of reason. And reason, which as we have all too often shown is the greatest of vices, is also innate. But in its original state it was not a vice, whereas as we find it and use it today, it is.

Moral Reaction

It's a commonplace that when we meet with resistance it only stimulates and builds up the strength needed to go on with and finish whatever we are trying to do. I'd like to add that often, if I'd have scored ten without resistance, I'll score fifteen or twenty with it. And this often through pure, determined willpower, rather than any mere excess of mechanical force due to overestimating the resistance and applying more strength than was necessary, as when meaning to push something from one place to another, you find at the first shove that it won't budge, increase the force applied and now the thing moves farther than you wanted. No, I mean willfully, on purpose: for example, I give a shove and nothing, another and still nothing, a third likewise, then I get angry, grab the thing in my hands and drag it far farther than I originally planned, so that now if I want to have it where it should be I'll have to take it back to the proper place, which I do. And the distance I dragged it is often double or even triple what I wanted. This happens because I stop thinking, I lose sight of the purpose of what I'm about—to move the thing to that particular place—now all I want is to overcome that resistance and take my revenge, show that my will and strength are greater than its will and strength, and the farther I move the thing the more I show that and the greater my victory and revenge; in short, with this new goal in our minds, that's what we strive for and achieve, and hence we hardly care that we're working against our original goal, which at this point in fact we've entirely forgotten about. Now I'll apply this physical case to the moral sphere.

Egoism a Common Cause—Barbarisms—Civilization. Process of Civilization—Egoism—Moral Handbook—Social Machiavellianism—Arrogance

L'orgueil nous sépare de la société: notre amour-propre nous donne un rang à part qui nous est toujours disputé: l'estime de soi-même qui se fait trop sentir est presque toujours punie par le mépris universel. [Pride separates us from society: our self-regard sets us in a class apart that others will always dispute: exaggerated and evident self-esteem is almost always punished with universal contempt]. Mme de Lambert, *Avis d'une mère à sa fille*, in *Oeuvres complètes*, quoted above (p. 633), p. 99, end. That's how things naturally are in society, that's how nature fashions this human institution; meant for the good and well-being of all, society can't really exist if the individual does not bring his own views, interests, goals, thoughts, opinions, feelings and affections, inclinations and actions more or less into line with those of others, if he insists, that is, on focusing all these energies on himself. The stronger the self in the individual the less society really exists. So if egoism is absolute, society will exist only in name. This because when each individual has no other goal than himself, paying no attention to the common good, and spending no thought or effort for the good or pleasure of others, then each individual will form a society on his own, separate and complete and perfectly distinct, just as his goal is perfectly distinct; so the world goes back to being what it was in the beginning, before the origin of society, which at this point is, both in fact and in substance, in its purpose and its essence, dissolved.

Enthusiasm — Poets — Excess Leads Nowhere — Intense Willfulness — Memories of My Life — Theory of the Arts. Practical Part

Very often excess, or too much of something, leads to nothing. The dialecticians note that something that proves too much actually proves nothing. But this property of excess is observable in ordinary life. An excess or surfeit of feelings leads to an inability to feel. It produces apathy and inertia, even a habit of inertia in individuals and peoples; in this regard see my comment agreeing with Mme de Staël, Florus, and others, pp. 620 bottom–625* top. At the height of passion's fervor a poet is a poet no more; he can't write poetry at this moment. In the presence of nature, his whole soul taken up with the image of the infinite, ideas thronging his mind, he is incapable of distinguishing, choosing, or grasping any of them: in short, he can't do anything or turn his feelings to any good: by any good I mean any consideration or aphorism, any use or piece of writing, any theory or practice. You can't express the infinite while you're feeling it, only afterward: and when the finest poets wrote lines that roused our sense of wonder for the infinite, their minds were not filled with any sensation of the infinite; conjuring up the infinite, they weren't feeling it.

*Florus, 4, 12, toward the end: *Hic finis Augusto bellicorum certaminum fuit: idem rebellandi finis Hispaniae. Certa mox fi des et aeterna pax; CUM IPSORUM INGENIO IN PACIS PARTES PROMPTIORE: tum consilio Caesaris.* [This was the end of Augustus's military campaigns and likewise of the Spanish uprising. Afterward loyalty and lasting peace prevailed, partly thanks to the character of the Spanish, more inclined to peace, and partly due to Caesar's shrewdness.] Having read everything Florus has to say about the fighting prowess of the Spanish, bk. 2, 17–18, bk. 3, 22, and in the same section mentioned above, immediately before the lines quoted (note that critics believe Florus was a native of Spain), where he recounts the famous siege of Sagunto; remembering too the place in Velleius where among many other reflections on the qualities of the Spanish he actually claims that Spain *in tantum Sertorium armis extulit, ut per quinquennium dijudicari non potuerit, Hispanis Romanisne in armis plus esset roboris, et uter populus alteri pariturus foret* [transformed Sertorius into such a powerful fighting phenomenon that for five years it was hard to predict whether Rome's or Spain's military might would prevail, or which of the two peoples would be dominated by the other] (bk. 2, 90, § 3), after reading all this and all the other endless accounts of Spanish valor, ancient and modern, it's astonishing that Florus speaks of the Spanish character and mindset as *promptius in pacis partes* [more inclined to peace]. But precisely this is the quality of southern peoples, something modern philosophical authors, especially foreign ones, all mention: a marked disposition both to activity and repose, just as ready to fight bravely and desperately as to enjoy the pleasures of peace and become attached to them, too attached, to the point of growing slack and inert. These peoples find so many resources in their imagination, climate, and nature that their life is always mentally busy, even when in practical terms it is indolent and empty. *Leur vie n'est qu'un rêve* [Their life is but a dream], says Mme de Staël.

This extreme mental activity can perfectly well lead them to extreme physical activity (in fact, to the only authentic kind of physical activity, one that springs directly from inner activity, as can be seen when you compare southern soldiers to northern ones, the northerners acting more like machines obedient to every impulse than living beings); but it can also exempt them from physical activity, making up for its absence, because southerners find life enough in their minds, in themselves as individuals. In fact, this quality very often works against practical physical activity, and hence an excess of inner life turns southerners into dreamers, makes them sluggish and overrelaxed (though in the right circumstances, they'll burst into busy action again, action that is the effect of enthusiasm and imagination, or is the stronger and livelier when it is; except where long habit has led whole peoples, the Italians for example, to descend into torpor). *Ailleurs, c'est la vie qui, telle qu'elle est, ne suffit pas aux facultés de l'âme; ici ce sont les facultés de l'âme qui ne suffisent pas à la vie, et la surabondance des sensations inspire une rêveuse indolence dont on se rend à peine compte en l'éprouvant.* [In other places it is life, such as it is, that isn't enough for the mental faculties; here—Staël is talking about the country around Naples—it is the mental faculties that can't deal with the intense life, and the excess of sensations induces a dreamy sluggishness you are barely aware of while you're experiencing it.] (Staël, *Corinne*, bk. 11, ch. 1, Paris 1812, 5th ed., tome 2, p. 176.) So it is with the Italians who were formidable in war in ancient times, and in modern times too, yet in conditions of peace are idle and sloppy in the extreme and show absolutely no interest in any novelty or change. So again the Spanish have been entirely peaceful over this past century, after being determinedly warlike and aggressive in the two centuries before, in the same way that in ancient times they were extremely combative, or at least very brave in defending themselves before the arrival of Augustus, then, as Florus tells us, endlessly peaceful and loyal afterward; and likewise at the beginning of this century they passed in a flash from a very long very deep sleep to a war we might describe as spontaneous, definitely national, very intense, general, and extremely cruel. Same thing with the French, brave in war and effeminate and flabby in peace.

It's just like children, and again this comes as an effect consequent on the same causes; they're naturally extremely active, but when circumstances prevent them from physical action, they compensate by filling their minds with a very lively inner activity. And by inner activity, whether we're talking about children or these southern peoples, I also mean the kind that manifests itself externally, but as an involvement in stupid, frivolous things, from which they draw enough life and food to keep their minds going; but being frivolous, such activity couldn't continue, couldn't happen at all, couldn't suffice for those engaged in it, were it not for the intensity of energy and imagination they put into it, in short, the strength of the mental faculties and the inner life.

Exactly the opposite occurs among northern peoples; if they want to have a life, they need activity and movement and novelty and external variety, since they have no other life, no internal activity. Hence though in appearance they may seem far more active than other peoples, in reality, if their natural tendencies and character get the upper hand, they are extremely lumpish.

Orientals, I believe, can be put in the same category as the southerners in this regard.

Sensibility. Emotion — Sensitive
People — Memories of My Life

A man who is imaginative, emotional, and full of enthusiasm, but not physically attractive, has more or less the same relation to nature as an ardent, sincere lover toward his beloved when his love is not requited. He goes eagerly toward nature, he deeply feels all its power, its fascination, its attractions, its beauty, he loves it rapturously, but just as if, as I said, this love were not requited, he feels he is not part of the beauty he loves and admires, he realizes he is excluded from the sphere of beauty, like a lover banished from the affections, caresses, and company of his beloved. After thoughts of nature and beauty and the feelings they arouse in him, he finds the return to himself is always painful. He instantly and constantly senses that this beauty he admires and loves and feels does not belong to him. He feels the same pain a man feels when he sees or thinks of his beloved in another man's arms, or in love with another, but absolutely cold toward him. It's almost as if beauty and nature were made not for him but for others (others — here's an even more unpleasant thought — less worthy than he is, people who don't deserve to enjoy beauty and nature at all, incapable as they are of feeling it and knowing it, etc.), and he feels the same disgust and subtle pain of the starving man who sees others eating daintily, abundantly, heartily, with no hope at all of ever doing the same. In short, he feels excluded, he knows he is, and that there's no hope, he cannot enjoy the favors of this divinity that nevertheless, to make matters worse, remains so present to him, so close that he almost feels it's inside him and he identifies with it — I mean abstract beauty, nature.

Objects of Compassion — Compassion — Sensitive People — Memories of My Life — Theory of the Arts. Practical Part

The unlucky man who isn't attractive — worse still if he's old — may attract sympathy, but not tears. That's as true in plays, poems, novels, etc., as in life.

Praise — Social Machiavellianism — Memories of My Life

Man is so eager for praise that even when it comes to activities he's never tried or cared to shine in, things he thinks are trivial, he's still pleased if someone does praise him. In fact, often the experience will prompt him to try to improve his opinion of this trifling thing he's been praised for, to convince himself that this activity, or the fact of his being praised for it, is no small matter in other people's heads.

Philosophical Thoughts — Injustice — Generosity — Revenge — Memories of My Life

When we witness an injustice, everyone wants to see it punished, but the best people want to punish it themselves.

Compassion — Weakness

In several places I've talked about compassion being aroused by weakness, but I should specify that this happens mostly in people who are strong and feel strong at that moment, this feeling being in contrast with the apparent weakness or helplessness of the object of their compassion or affection: the object becomes lovable, in fact, thanks to the compassion, even when the object is not suffering or perhaps has never suffered nor ever come to harm as a result of his weakness. British Bards had something to say on the matter in some lines that go like this: "To suffer with patience and generosity is a sure sign of courage and sublime spirit; while to abuse one's strength is a sign of cowardly cruelty" (*Annali di scienze e lettere,* loc. cit., p. 932 (p. 378)). When someone is strong, but generous with it, his sense of his strength naturally and effortlessly gives rise to feelings of compassion for other people's weaknesses, and so to *a certain willingness to love, and a certain readiness to respond and to find another lovable, and this quality is more marked in such a person than in others.* They tend always to be patient with weaker people, rather than dominating them, even when it might make sense to do so.

Self-Regard — Misfortunes — Memories of My Life

One of the main reasons why unhappiness makes people inept, weakens and unnerves them, and saps their strength is simply that unhappiness undermines our self-regard. I'm mainly talking about the kind of serious, long-term unhappiness that wages a constant war of attrition against the sufferer's self-regard, a determined, violent struggle that forces him into a state entirely contrary to the aims, goals, and desires of his self-regard, finally wearing it down until he becomes less generous toward himself, if only because inured to feeling unhappy, despite all his efforts to resist. In fact, if this kind of unhappiness doesn't reduce a man to deep desperation, suicide, and self-hatred, the highest level and most intense form of self-regard in the circumstances, it must necessarily reduce him to the opposite state, to coldness and a lack of interest toward himself; since if he went on being as violently opposed to himself as he was initially, how could he bear life, or accept to go on living, seeing, and feeling the object of his intense self-regard, indeed of his whole life in every respect, always unhappy?

But self-regard is the only possible spring of human feeling and action, whatever the goal, good or evil, noble or otherwise. So when the elasticity and strength of this spring is diminished and depressed, shrunk to the limit (I mean the lowest point compatible with life), then a man is no longer capable of action, or strong, lively feeling, etc., toward either himself or others, since even when it is a question of feelings for others, of making sacrifices and so on, there's no other force can drive a man but his self-regard, applied and directed to this end. So the man who has inevitably grown cold toward himself, cold toward everything, is reduced to a state of physical and moral inaction. And the fact that self-regard has been weakened, self-regard in its radical form (not insofar as directed to this or that goal), the *real* weakening, I mean, of this love of self, is the reason why virtue, enthusiasm, heroism, and generosity are weakened too, all the things that at first glance would seem to be opposed to self-regard and to require self-regard to be cut down to size so that they could emerge and triumph, the things that seem most hampered and damaged by the strength of self-regard. Thus this decline in self-regard dries up the wellsprings of poetry and the imagination; loving himself no longer, or very little, man no longer loves nature either; not feeling his own emotions, he doesn't feel nature or the effects of its beauty, etc. A dense fog of indifference, immediate cause of inertia and insensitivity, settles on his whole spirit and all his faculties, this from the moment that he becomes cold, or barely alive to the object *that alone is able to interest him* and move him morally and physically in any way at all toward all the other objects, I mean himself.

Self-Regard — Misfortunes — Memories of My Life

The above considerations allow us to generalize and simplify our idea of the system of human behavior, or our theory of man, by making clear how in every respect and in all possible circumstances of life, the unique principle of self-regard is at work, and how all effects of human life will be in proportion to the greater or lesser strength, greater or lesser weakness and particular direction of this one motivator: however much such effects might at first glance appear to be the result of quite other causes.

Firearms — Courage

Aside from other effects noted elsewhere in these thoughts, the invention and use of firearms has greatly diminished the courage of soldiers and of men in general. *La victoire . . . s'obtient aujourd'hui par la regularité et la précision des manoeuvres, souvent sans en venir aux mains. Nos guerres ne se décident plus guère que de loin, à coups de canon et de fusil; et nos timides fantassins, sans armes défensives, effrayés par le bruit et l'effet de nos armes à feu, n'osent plus s'aborder: les combats à l'armes blanches sont devenus fort rares.* [These days victory is achieved by organizing precise maneuvers, often without arriving at physical combat. Our wars are decided for the most part from a distance, with canon and rifle shot;

and our fearful infantry, terrified by the noise and efficiency of our firearms and having no weapons with which to defend themselves, no longer dares engage battle directly: combat with sword and spear has become extremely rare.] Thus Baron Rogniat in *Considérations sur l'art de la guerre*, Paris, published by Firmin Didot, 1817, Introduction, p. 1. And like the soldiers, other men are doing the same, using firearms instead of swords, reducing every battle, public or private, to a question of catching people unawares, shooting from a distance, without ever fighting hand to hand; all this quite apart from the influence of military education and of the nature of war on the entire nation. I shall have to read the whole of Baron Rogniat's book since it gives very clear explanations of the art of war together with a great deal of philosophy as well as frequent parallels between the ancients and the moderns and between various peoples, applying the science of human behavior to this particular art. There's no doubt war is a proper subject for the philosopher, partly because it gives rise to some of the greatest and most important upheavals, and then for its connections with endless ramifications of theories of society, man, and living creatures in general.

Courage — Euphemisms of the Ancients

If we sing when we're afraid, it is not to keep ourselves company, as people commonly suppose, nor for pure and simple distraction, but (as I find very incisively and subtly expressed in Magalotti's second letter against the Atheists) to demonstrate and convince ourselves that we are not afraid. This observation could perhaps be applied to lots of things and lead to many other reflections. It's already clear that when we see trouble coming, we try to fool ourselves into thinking it isn't trouble, or not such bad trouble, and we look for other people who are, or seem to be, convinced of this, or as a last resort we pretend to be already convinced, behaving and talking among ourselves as if we were. And that's what happens with the kind of singing mentioned above. In fact, a great many people have the habit of talking down the troubles hanging over them and imagining them less serious than they are, consoling themselves and bracing themselves this way, looking for courage not by going to meet their trouble, spurning it as they should, but by imagining it's not real or not important, which is why so many people are never or only very rarely dismayed, because when someone warns them of something, or they see it coming themselves, first they don't believe it at all (I mean they deny or decry all the reasons for believing it), so that if the trouble doesn't actually materialize they haven't been afraid, while others maybe have, and with reason; next they minimize it as far as they possibly can, and hence are actually afraid only in those rare situations where trouble is so real and evident and touches them in such an immediate way that they simply can't deny it, because otherwise even when trouble does turn up, they will often refuse to believe it is trouble; I mean they don't want to believe it. These people, who often pass for courageous perhaps, are actually the most cowardly of all; not only are they unable to deal with real trouble, they can't even deal with the idea of trouble, and when they become aware of some major problem hanging over them, or that's actually happened, they immediately and determinedly dig themselves in to deny it, withdrawing and taking spineless refuge in telling themselves over and over again that it's nothing.

So that when real trouble puts them to the test, everybody can see what cowards they are, going crazy, despairing, throwing fits like little girls, yelling and weeping and pleading, all things I've seen and observed myself in someone I know and was naturally bound to know extremely well, and who fits the picture painted above in every detail. But then, sadly, it's plain that man does have a propensity for denial, for pretending as best he can that trouble isn't there, hence the εὐφημία [using words of good omen] of the ancient Greeks, who would give unpleasant things (τὰ δεινὰ) names aimed at hiding or disguising their unpleasantness (see Helladius in Meurs), something they certainly weren't doing just to ward off bad luck. And even in Italian one says, *se Dio facesse altro di me* [if God were to do something else with me], meaning, *if I died* (see the Crusca dictionary under *altro*), and in Latin likewise, *si quid humanum paterer, mihi accideret, etc.* [if something human should happen to me], and so on in hundreds of other situations.

Love—Pleasure, Theory of—Hope—Vagueness

From my theory of pleasure it follows that man, always desiring as he does an infinite and entirely satisfying pleasure, is constantly desiring and hoping for something he cannot mentally conceive. And so it is. All human desires and hopes even for the most specific things, pleasures rather, things already enjoyed on other occasions even, are never absolutely clear and distinct and precise, but always contain a confused idea, always refer to an object only confusedly conceived. This is why hope is better than pleasure, having as it does that quality of being undefined which reality cannot have. This is most obvious in love, where the mind's activity, passion, and life are more intense than ever and hence the desires and hopes involved are similarly more sensitive and lively and come to the fore more powerfully than in other circumstances. Now notice how on the one hand the desires and hopes of the person who's really in love are more confused, vague, and indefinite than the hopes animated by any other passion: and it is typical of love (something many have observed) that it presents us with an idea that is infinite (I mean more *perceptibly* indefinite than the ideas that other passions present) and one that we are less able to conceive than other ideas, etc. On the other hand, note that precisely because of this quality of infinity, something inseparable from true love, this passion with all its stormy ups and downs, is the source of the greatest pleasures man can experience.

Philosophical Thoughts—Pleasure, Theory of— Memories—Hope—Memories of My Life

The memory of pleasure may be compared with hope and produces more or less the same effects. Like hope it's more of a pleasure than pleasure itself; it is far sweeter remembering a pleasure (never really experienced, but that at a distance we have the impression of having experienced) than enjoying it; just as it is sweeter to look forward to it, since from a distance you have the impression you can taste it already. Distance works in our favor in both situations; hence you might come to the conclusion that the worst time of our lives is the moment of pleasure and enjoyment.

Satirical Thoughts—Negligence, Inactivity—Time—
Handbook of Practical Philosophy—Memories of My Life

People who never do anything and as a result have more free time for doing things are usually less likely than anyone else to find the time to do a chore, even if it's something they really want to do, or to remember something that needs doing, some job they've been given and that, again, they really want to get done. The opposite is true of people whose days are full and who have less free time and more things to remember. The reason is obvious: habit, the habit of being lazy, and the habit of being busy. You can see the same opposite effects of habit in the same person who in one period develops a habit of inactivity and negligence and in another a habit of activity and diligence.

Love—Women—Grace—Social Machiavellianism—
Memories of My Life

One of the most common and sure ways of being a success with the women is to mock them and talk them down and so on, a fact we can partly ascribe to that charm generated by things that are extraordinary, though it's also the result of the sort of contrast that gives us piquancy, and again of the way our self-regard is set in motion by mockery, so that we yearn for the respect of someone talking us down, and yearn all the more precisely because that respect seems hard to get. The same is true of men when they meet women who mock them or act coy.

Self-Regard—Envy—Hatred of Our Peers

Envy, a very natural passion, and according to Holy Scripture the first vice of the first son of man, is an effect and a manifest sign of the natural hatred of man toward man, in society, however imperfect and small that society may be. For we envy others even for having things we already have, in fact we envy them more intensely over these things; we envy people for having things even when their having them doesn't harm us in the slightest; we envy them for having things that it's absolutely impossible for us to have, things it wouldn't even be in our interest to have; and finally, we almost envy them for things we don't ourselves want, things we wouldn't take even if they were offered. So really it's the other person's well-being, pure and simple, the mere sight of his presumed happiness that is in itself difficult for us to take, and naturally so; it's that well-being that is the object of this passion, which as a result can derive only from our hatred of others, which again derives from our self-regard, but derives, if I may be allowed to put it like this, the same way theologians say the person of the Word proceeds from the Father, and the Holy Spirit from both; that is, there never was a moment in which the Father existed when the Word and the Holy Spirit didn't.

Self-Regard—Envy—Hatred of Our Peers

Why is favoritism always hateful and intolerable, even when the person favoring or helping someone more than others isn't depriving those others of their due, or of anything he would otherwise have given them, in fact isn't doing them harm in any way at all? Because of the natural hatred of man toward man, something inseparable from our self-regard. On this subject, see the Gospel parable of the householder and the laborers in the vineyard.*

    *I've already mentioned an infertile woman who beat a pregnant horse complaining, *You pregnant and me not?* I think that it's unlikely a cripple can take pleasure in his healthy children and not feel a certain impulse to hate them, or a difficulty loving them, something that can easily turn into hatred, and then will be stupidly dubbed revulsion, as if this were an innate passion without a moral cause. One could give endless examples of this phenomenon, like the hatred of ugly mothers for their pretty daughters, the way they torment and pester entirely innocent girls, without the girls' or even their understanding why. Same thing with dumb or just unlucky fathers toward a son who is very smart or who enjoys advantages they didn't. Same thing (and this is extremely common) with the old toward the young (even their own children (no, especially their own children), boys and girls alike, etc.); this whenever the old haven't given up on the desires of youth and the young, entirely innocent and good as they may be, don't behave as if they were old. Same with brothers and sisters, and so on and so on. The self-regard that is inseparable from living creatures very naturally produces, almost turns into, hatred of others, even those nature has most commended to us (to our very self-regard) and made dearest to us.

Moral Etiquette—Envy—Social Machiavellianism—Hatred of Our Peers

The sight of a happy man, full of some good luck he's had, or even just moderately cheered by it, some promotion won or favor granted, etc., is almost always extremely irksome not just to people who are upset or depressed, or simply not prone to joyfulness, whether out of choice or habit, but even to people neither happy nor sad and not at all harmed or deflated by this success. Even when it comes to friends and close relatives it's the same. So that the man who has reason to be happy will either have to hide his pleasure, or be casual and amusing about it, as if it hardly mattered; otherwise, his presence and conversation will prove hateful and tiresome, even to people who ought to be happy about his good luck or who have no reason at all to be upset by it. This is what thoughtful, well-educated people do, people who know how to control themselves. What can all this mean but that our self-regard inevitably and without our noticing leads us to hate our fellow man? There's no doubt that in situations like this, even the nicest people with nothing at all to gain or lose from another's success, will need to get a grip on themselves and show a certain heroism to join in the partying, or merely not to feel depressed by it.

Man's Inclinations—Hope and Fear

Another thing that shows we're more inclined to fear than hope is the fact that we're generally very ready to believe in what we fear but less so in what we hope for, even if it's more likely to happen. And given two people of whom one fears and another hopes that the same thing will happen, the first will believe in it happening and the second won't. And if we switch from fearing something to hoping for it, we find we're no longer able to believe in a thing we previously found it impossible not to believe in, an experience I've been through any number of times. And given two things, either opposite or simply different, one desired and the other feared and both equally likely to happen, our conviction will latch on to the latter and shun the former. Examining the grounds for certain propositions that I initially feared but later hoped were true, I first found them extremely persuasive and later entirely unfounded.

Man and His Assumptions

A man living in isolation would naturally, albeit confusedly perhaps, assume that the world was made for him alone. Meantime, men in general assume that it is made for the whole human species, since this is something they live in the midst of and are entirely familiar with, basing their conclusions readily and complacently on the data that society and common knowledge offer them. But because they can't live in society with all creatures, their reasoning stops here, and without the sort of reflection that few people are capable of, they don't arrive at the realization that the world is made for all the creatures on the planet. I've seen men who have lived a long time in the world, then withdrawn into solitude, men who were always self-centered, who believed in good faith that the world was more or less meant entirely for themselves, a belief evident in everything they did and implicit in all they said. Not only was suffering, or just not getting whatever they wanted, unthinkable for them, but even the idea that anyone or anything might not be always and entirely at their service was unimaginable; and when this happened, they showed their amazement and indignation in ways that were quite remarkable, and sometimes even incredible for people accustomed to polite company and the sort of concessions society demands, an etiquette they actually took great pride in. But they never realized that by behaving like this they were letting others down, or demanding more than was appropriate.

Philosophical Thoughts — Cheerfulness — Handbook of Practical Philosophy — Memories of My Life

Intense action of a kind we're not used to, always, or almost always, puts us in a cheerful mood, so long as it isn't physically exhausting.

Consolation — Regret — Manual of Practical Philosophy

In a previous entry I said that regret — our not being able to pretend that something that has gone wrong isn't our fault — increases our suffering by about half; but it also increases our unhappiness over losing out on something, or just not having it, to the same degree; very often, in fact, regret is the sole cause of our unhappiness; we wouldn't feel unhappy at all if we didn't think it was our fault that we didn't have this thing, if we hadn't had a chance to acquire it at all, for example. I tried to find a voice for this human emotion that people feel, or you expect them to feel, whenever some opportunity presents itself, and that encourages and even compels us to take advantage of such opportunities, almost in spite of ourselves, in my [pastoral tragedy] *Telesilla*. Very often a missed opportunity can leave us extremely upset over not having something, even when it was not our fault we didn't get it and when previously we hadn't been worried about this thing at all. On these occasions it's a standard mental reaction to look for consolation by trying to convince ourselves that we are absolutely not to blame for having missed out on the opportunity and that it couldn't really have led to anything anyway, actually it would quite definitely have led to nothing, and so was hardly an opportunity at all, and so on.

Courage—Youth—Old People—Physical Strength

Aside from other effects noted in previous entries, physical strength, even when it doesn't last long, makes people more than usually courageous and less susceptible to fear, even in the presence of extraordinary dangers and the like. This is why the young are more courageous than the old, and careless of their lives, even though they have so much more to lose, etc. This in contrast with that old observation that the main source of courage is having little to lose, etc.

Self-Regard—Love—Social Machiavellianism

There's no better way of impressing a proud, disdainful young woman and getting your way with her, than putting her down. Now who would have thought that self-regard (since it's only from self-love that love for another can spring) would react like this; that when it is stung, you would feel attracted to the person doing the stinging? Who wouldn't rather have supposed that a proud woman in love with herself needed to be won over by showing interest and wearing her down with constant attention, constant praise, and so on? But that's how it is. Not only will praise and attention lead her to look down on you more than she already did, but if you've managed to get her attention by putting her down, so that she begins to show some interest in you, and then, out of love, or weakness, or because you think you've done enough, whatever, you try to win her over with more natural ways and you give her the slightest sign of submission, of a love that really is love, you'll have thrown it all away and she will immediately be disgusted and despise you. What you have to do is go on regardless, showing no interest in her right to the end. And this is a very simple consequence of our multiform self-regard that produces all kinds of effects, many of them counterintuitive. So much so that while almost all women can be won over by putting them down (though sometimes and in some circumstances, they do take offense), nevertheless the more intense and tyrannical their self-regard is, the more arrogant and self-centered they are, so the more this will be true. See in this regard Duclos's *Mémoires secrets*, Lausanne 1791, tome 1, p. 95, and pp. 271–273. See also another entry where I noticed this effect when talking about attraction and piquancy. For sure, this metamorphosis of self-regard is hardly one of the most natural, though it's not so far from nature. It requires a rather twisted personality, but one that is all too common.

Childhood—Children—Illusions—Pleasure, Theory of—Science and Ignorance—Vagueness— Handbook of Practical Philosophy

The human mind is such that it gets much more satisfaction from a small pleasure—that is, from the idea of a feeling that may be small but whose limits remain unclear—than from a larger one whose limits can be seen and felt. Hoping on a small enjoyment or advantage is a much greater pleasure than actually possessing a much larger one that has already been experienced (if something hasn't yet actually been experienced, it remains in the category of hope). Science destroys the main pleasures of our minds because it establishes facts and fixes borders, although in so many fields, materially speaking, it has enormously broadened our ideas. I say materially, rather than spiritually, because, for example, the distance of the sun from the earth was far greater in the human mind when people believed it was a few miles away, but didn't know how many, than now that we know exactly how many thousands of miles away it is. Thus science is hostile to the greatness of ideas, despite the fact that it has vastly extended natural opinions. It has extended them as clear ideas, but a tiny confused idea is always bigger than a huge one that is absolutely clear. Uncertainty as to whether something really exists or not is a source of greatness that is destroyed by the certainty that it really does exist. The notion of the Antipodes was so much greater when Petrarch said that maybe they existed than the same notion became the day we knew they did. What I say of science is true of experience too. The most important, no, the only greatness that man can confusedly feel fulfilled in is indeterminate greatness, something that also emerges from my theory of pleasure. Hence ignorance, which alone can hide the limits of things, is the principal source of indefinite ideas and suchlike. Hence it is also the greatest wellspring of happiness, and hence childhood is the happiest time of man's life, the most satisfying in itself and the least subject to boredom. Experience necessarily reveals the limits of many things, even for the natural man not engaged in society.

Weakness—Charm—Of Nature—
Theory of the Arts. Speculative Part

I've written a lot about the beauty that derives from weakness. It's a beauty that springs from pure inclination, and hence has nothing to do with ideal beauty; on the contrary, it lies outside the theory of beauty. Indeed, it's entirely relative. Leaving aside the endless other areas where weakness is a disadvantage and regrettable, notice that men like weakness in a woman, because it is natural to them, while women like strength and the impression of strength in a man. Strength in a woman is ugly, as is weakness in men. Except that sometimes a touch of masculinity in a woman and of femininity in a man creates contrast and imparts charm (but this precisely because it is unusual and unexpected).

Upbringing. Teaching—Youth—Man's
Inclinations—Memories of My Life

How far people are incorrigibly inclined to measure others against themselves one can see even in the most practical folk in the world. If, for example, they are extremely moral, it doesn't matter how much they know, feel, and see, they just can't convince themselves in their hearts that morality no longer exists and that these days it just doesn't figure among the motives that guide the human spirit. They may acknowledge this in the end, and say it too; in a fit of misanthropy they may even believe it, but as one believes momentarily in an intense and commonly shared illusion, while they'll never really be convinced of it in the core of their intellect. (Leave aside the young who are usually virtuous and who won't even accept that virtue is rare until experience shows them otherwise.) Likewise vice versa, etc., etc., etc. Example, my father.

Compassion—Interest in Others—
Hope—Memories of My Life

Someone who has lost any hope of being happy can't think of another's happiness, because you can't promote happiness except in respect to your own. So this person can't even be interested in another's unhappiness.

Beauty, Sign of Goodness—Civilization. Process of
Civilization—Compassion—Egoism—Physiognomy.
Eyes—Of Nature—Memories of My Life

Beauty naturally goes hand in hand with virtue. Without long experience men can't get used to the idea that a pretty face might hide an evil mind. And they're right, because nature has established a real correspondence between the interior and exterior, and if the two don't match up, it's usually because they've changed from what they naturally were. Still, there's no doubt that good-looking people are for the most part mean. The same goes for other natural and acquired advantages. Those who have them are hardly nice. An ugly man, with no qualities or advantages, is more likely to move toward the good side. People with no talents are usually nicer than those blessed with many. And all this is very natural in society. A person grows proud of the advantage he knows he has over others and tries to make the most of it. If he is strong, he'll use his strength. The weakest folk toe the line and do whatever is convenient and desirable to others, to ingratiate themselves. Strong people don't need to do this. So much for the abuse of advantages. An inevitable and entirely predictable abuse, given society. This is my position on powerful people and so on; they just can't be virtuous. When it comes to individuals, my experience is you don't find real friendliness, real and regular kindness and easy manners, interest in the good of others, and so on, except in people who are ugly or at some disadvantage; they were born into the servant class maybe and got used to it as children, though later rose out of it, or they are or were poor, or unlucky in some way.

Let me ask this then: is it or is it not an advantage to be beautiful, talented, etc., etc.? Virtue, etc., decorum, etc., etc., are or are not things nature promotes? (Definitely yes, because children and young people are always drawn to them.) What kind of strange paradox is it, then, that when we're organized in society these natural and acquired advantages become almost totally incompatible with good behavior? That if you want good behavior you have to hope you'll be dealing with someone ugly or dumb, etc., etc.? or even that the majority of people, or all of them, if that were possible, were ugly or dumb, for the sake of mankind? (Religious people often call these and suchlike disadvantages, favors and blessings from God.) What does all this mean if not that life in society is in contradiction with nature, and with itself? Since society itself can't go on without virtue and morality, which constitute the only ties between men and the only sufficient guarantee of order and society, etc., and that virtue and morality cannot coexist with something else equally necessary to the good of society, that is to say, individual advantages and benefits. What goes for individuals goes for nations too. We all know that justice, etc., etc., is generally observed by weak, poor, whatever, nations and leaders, and completely ignored by the others and indeed by the same weak and poor nations as soon as they achieve strength and riches, as happened with Rome.

Compassion

It's true that someone who's happy will not tend to be very compassionate, but it's also true that, no matter how sensitive he may have been at birth, someone really unhappy is almost totally incapable of spontaneous, sensitive compassion. Develop this truth in its various aspects, and causes.

Delicacy of Shapes—Charm—Of Nature—
Theory of the Arts. Speculative Part

The observations above offer a further, important demonstration that our ideas of beauty are relative and changeable; far from being based on some stable model, they depend on habits that change with circumstances. Today the idea of beauty is almost interchangeable with an idea of delicacy. A strapping peasant, man or woman, will not seem beautiful to people living in town. To our mind, the beautiful cannot include anything coarse. If there is coarseness (except in cases where its very incongruity and unseemliness produce a certain charm), then as far as we're concerned there is no beauty, or at least no perfect beauty. Now, there's no doubt that primitive man saw things quite differently, because all primitive men were coarse. There simply weren't any of the shapes we now call beautiful (you can see this with savages; they feel beauty just as much as we do, but not our beauty): and if there had been, they would have been ugly and pronounced ugly. So there's no room for delicacy in natural man's idea of beauty. Hence our present idea of beauty is not at all natural, quite the opposite in fact. Yet to us it seems completely natural, confusing as we do the natural with the spontaneous: because this idea of beauty comes to us spontaneously, unmediated by our will, but prompted by our mental habits.

It's quite likely that while today the basis or universal condition of beauty is delicacy, for primitive man it was what we call coarseness; because our present state and mental habits and ideas are, in this particular regard, exactly opposite to those of natural and primitive men and women. But if by chance delicacy did creep into the primitive idea of the beautiful, whether because unusual, and hence charming, or in some other way, it was a quite different delicacy than the one we reckon indispensable to beauty today. It was less delicate than our delicacy, to the point that we would find it close to being coarse and even rough. And vice versa our present delicacy would have seemed excessive, out of place and ugly to primitive man. In short the idea of delicacy could perhaps have crept into the way primitive man conceived beauty (especially the way man conceived it with regard to woman, since delicacy is natural for women and hence not out of place, but I mean a delicacy relative to, in proportion to, and in line with the different nature of primitive man, etc.), but only as I've described. So all beauty is relative. And there are differences between the beauty of the ancients and the beauty of the moderns, differences proportionate to the differences between these two societies, and again between beauty in one nation and in another; one climate and another, one century and another; between the beauty of the Italians and the beauty of the French, etc., etc.*

> *What emerges from all this is that man as he is today would not appreciate man as he was in the natural state, nor find him attractive; that natural ideas (ideas arising from nature, that is) about human beauty (thus the least susceptible to differences of opinion) are totally out of line with our own: that in particular the most beautiful woman imaginable in natural man's conception of beauty would not be at all attractive to modern man. Because the basis of human beauty is vital energy, which as it was in natural man would seem wrong and unattractive to modern woman, but because the natural man had too much of it, not too little. Yet since the basis of female beauty today is delicacy, we would find that there was too little of that in the natural state. And since so-called coarseness is typical of both man and woman in the natural state, this would be less of a problem (as we see things) in the man than the woman, because in the woman it would be farther from the basic attributes of her beauty than it would be in the man, etc., etc., etc.

Civilization. The Process of Civilization — Egoism — Youth — Sensitivity. Feeling — Sensitive People — Memories of My Life

It seems absurd, but perhaps the person most likely to fall into a state of apathy and insensitivity (and hence into the cruelty that comes from a coldness of character) is the person who is most sensitive, full of enthusiasm and inner life, and this in proportion precisely to his sensitivity. Particularly if he is unlucky in life; and especially in these times when the outer life of the world does not correspond to, or feed or offer any material to the inner life, where virtue and heroism are dead and a man of feeling and imagination and enthusiasm is quickly stripped of his illusions. The outer life of the ancients was so intense and drew great spirits so completely into its vortex that it was more likely to submerge them than to run dry. Today the kind of man I'm talking about burns his life up in a flash, precisely because of his extraordinary sensitivity. Then he's left empty, profoundly and permanently disillusioned, because he has already profoundly and intensely experienced everything: he didn't stay on the surface, or go a little deeper a bit at a time, he went right to the bottom, embraced everything, and then rejected it all, because it turned out to be unworthy and frivolous: now there is nothing left for him to see, or try, or hope. So it is that mediocre spirits, and people who are sensitive and alive up to a point, keep going for much longer, their whole lives even, preserving their sensitivity, always susceptible to affection, capable of caring for others and making sacrifices for them, not happy with the world, but hoping to be so, ready to open up to the idea of virtue and to believe it still matters, etc. (They haven't yet lost hope of happiness.) While those great spirits I mentioned, even as young people are already falling into apathy, listlessness, coldness, and a mortal, irremediable insensitivity that produces an uncaring egoism, a complete inability to love, and so on. That's how mental fervor and sensitivity are, if the mind doesn't find sustenance in the world around, they burn themselves up, and destroy themselves and are lost in no time, leaving a man as far beneath an ordinary generosity of spirit as previously he was above it. But a mediocre sensitivity survives, because it doesn't need much sustenance. So it is that this is not an age for *great* virtues.

Courage — Desperation — Resignation — Excess Produces Nothing — Theory of the Arts. Practical Part

I've said elsewhere that excess produces nothing, and mentioned excessive emotions and extreme adversities, the inevitable and present danger that gives a mental strength and calm even to the most cowardly, some unavoidable calamity that is just bound to happen, etc., situations that produce not so much agitation as paralysis and stupidity, a sort of unreasoning resignation, so that people's faces in these circumstances look very much as if they didn't care about what was happening at all: and a good painter would paint them looking very much like the most unconcerned, etc., man in the world, except for an air of stupefied rumination, the eyes gazing nowhere in particular. Let me add now that this doesn't apply to the sphere of action alone, but to the whole habit of not caring, of resignation to chance, insensitivity, etc., a state that arises from extreme unhappiness and habitual desperation, etc.

Moral Handbook — Envy — Hatred of Our Peers

The sight of other people taking intense pleasure in something in our presence is always irksome and prompts us to find such people hateful. So it's only prudent and polite not to show pleasure in the presence of others or to behave with a certain nonchalance that suggests it's hardly important and so on. The same holds for any advantages a person enjoys. See also my entry on kissing and cuddling the wife in the presence of others, and the way the English behave in this regard, which I've written about elsewhere, something Italians find really obnoxious too and that I've heard condemned as unbearable in a married couple who got into heavy petting in the presence of others. So it's true that man naturally hates man. Except when we ourselves intentionally procured someone the pleasure they're enjoying, in which case it reflects on us in a way and assists our ambitions, etc., in short we enjoy the pleasure too. This particular hatred is mostly experienced with our peers and superiors (less with inferiors, children, and so on); but above all with our peers and with friends and close acquaintances in particular, because the emotion most at work among these groups is envy, and we feel our inferiority intensely in whatever department it may emerge. Superiors are the object of a more general hatred that extends to their entire person and condition, etc., and has less to do with the details, or is less sensitive to them, if only because one can hardly compete with such people when it comes to pleasures, etc. Equally in the case of inferiors, their advantages or pleasures would have to be considerable (though in that case our hatred toward them is greater than toward anyone else) before they could offend our self-regard or whip up our jealousy, etc. All the same it's true that we always feel a certain distaste.

Grief—Of Nature

The grief natural man feels is extremely intense, as is evident from the decisions and actions it inspires, and inspired among the ancients. All the same, one sees and admires among country folk how extremely unusual it is for them not just to prolong their grief over time, something natural only to the most vehement passions, but even to conceive it and feel it intensely and shake themselves out of their normal unfeeling state. They arrange the funerals of their wives and children, they take their dead to church, watch them being buried, and are laughing a moment later; they talk about it without emotion, rarely shed a tear, even though, if grief does hit them, it is exactly the grief of people close to nature. And not just country folk; all the poorer people and the working classes react the same way. Which shows how merciful nature is because, yes, it gives natural men extremely intense, very regular, and very easily procured pleasures, and though making them in consequence subject to extraordinary intensity in their grief, it doesn't, as you might have supposed, condemn them to experiencing grief frequently, even at the lower level of intensity that educated people experience it so often. On the one hand the coarseness of their hearts and the fact that the faculties that give rise to grief, their sensitivity and so on, haven't developed (or rather haven't undergone an analogous alteration); and on the other the constant and intense distraction which basic needs and hard work create for natural man, etc., etc., their being quite used to certain troubles, etc., prevent them from grieving too easily, and inure them to life's hardships, making them more inclined to enjoy than to suffer, ready to forget the bad things, unable to feel them deeply, except on rare occasions, and so on. Educated people who are regularly or extraordinarily busy are in the same position. Likewise those who've experienced a lot of bad luck.

Love of Country—Self-Regard—Egoism—Envy—Hatred
of Our Peers—Foreigners—Memories of My Life

Someone who has given up hope for himself or who, for whatever reason, loves himself less intensely will be less envious of his
peers and hate them less than others and hence in this respect be
more open to friendship or at least experience less contradiction
in friendship. Someone who loves himself more is less able to love
others. Apply these observations to nations, to the way different
levels of love of one's country are always proportional to different
levels of hatred of other countries; to the need to make man selfish
on behalf of his country so that he can love his peers for his own
sake, pretty much as the theologians say that he must love himself
and his neighbors in God and for the love of God.

Friendship—Egoism—Youth—Envy—Hatred
of Our Peers—Old Age—Memories of My Life

Man's hatred of man mainly manifests itself between persons
of the same profession, etc., and is confirmed by what happens between such people. For example, granted that perfect friendship,
abstractly considered, is impossible and contradictory to human nature, between peers even ordinary friendship becomes extremely
difficult, rare and inconstant, etc. Schiller, a man of great feeling,
was hostile to Goethe (not only are people of the same profession
not friends with each other, or less friendly, but there is actually
more hatred between them than between others who are not in the
same circumstances) etc., etc., etc. Women enjoy the troubles of
other women, even their best friends'. Young people the troubles of

the young, and so on. See *Corinne*, tome 3, pp. 365 ff., bk. 20, ch. 4. So we find less friendship and more hatred not just among people in the same profession but in the same age group, etc., etc. Except in cases where they build illusions together, something that does much to foster friendship among young people, there is no doubt, especially now that the great and beautiful illusions are no longer with us, that friendships are more likely to form between an older or mature person and a younger than between two young people; and again between two older people rather than two younger; because these days, with the old illusions gone, and virtue nowhere to be found among the young, older people are more likely to be less enamored of themselves than the young, to be weary of their egoism, because disenchanted with the world, and hence more likely to love others.

So it's true that virtue, as Cicero claimed in *De amicitia*, is the basis of friendship and that there can be no friendship without virtue, because virtue is nothing other than the opposite of egoism, which is the main obstacle to friendship, etc., etc., etc.

Courage — Physical Strength — Wine — Memories of My Life

Physical vitality, whether steady or fleeting, gives a man a powerful sense of self and has him imagining himself superior to things, other people and nature itself; it prompts him to defy the consequence of calamities, persecution, dangers, injustice, etc., etc.; it fills him with courage, etc., etc.; in short, a vigorous man feels and believes himself master of the world and himself, and truly a man.

Boredom—Memories of My Life

Boredom is the most sterile of human passions. Born of emptiness and generating the void, because not just sterile in itself, but making everything it touches or mixes with sterile too, etc.

Illusions—Opinions (Diversity of)—Reason

The power of nature and the weakness of reason. I've said elsewhere that for opinions to have a real influence on people they must take the form of passions. So long as man has anything natural about him, he will be more passionate about opinion than about his passions. One could quote endless examples to demonstrate this point. But since all opinions that aren't, or don't seem to be, prejudices will have only pure reason to support them, in the ordinary way of things they are completely powerless to influence men. Religious people (even today, and maybe more these days than ever before, *in reaction to the opposition they meet*) are more passionate about their religion than their other passions (to which religion is hostile); they sincerely hate people who are not religious (though they pretend not to) and would make any sacrifice to see their system triumph (actually they already do this, mortifying inclinations that are natural and contrary to religion), and they feel intense anger whenever religion is humbled or contested. Nonreligious people, on the other hand, so long as their not being religious is simply the result of a coolheaded conviction, or of doubt, don't hate religious people and wouldn't make sacrifices for their unbelief, etc., etc. So it is that hatred over matters of opinion is never reciprocal, except in those cases where for both sides the opinion is a prejudice, or takes that form. There's no war then between prejudice and reason, but only between prejudice and prejudice, or rather, only prejudice has the will to fight, not reason. The wars, hostilities, and hatreds over opinions, so frequent in ancient times, right up to the present day in fact, wars both public and private, between parties, sects, schools, orders, nations, individuals—wars which naturally made people determined enemies of anyone who held an opinion different from their own—only happened because pure reason never found any place in their opinions, they were all just prejudices, or took that form, and hence were really passions. Poor philosophy, then, that people talk so much about and place so much trust in these days. She can be sure no one will fight for her, though her enemies will fight her with ever greater determination; and the less philosophy influences the world and reality, the greater her progress will be, I mean the more she purifies herself and distances herself from prejudice and passion. So never hope for anything from philosophy or the reasonableness of this century.

Love—Youth—Charm—Social Machiavellianism

A man famous for his profligacy, debauchery, amorous conquests, and infidelity in love makes a big impression on the ladies with this fame alone, but perhaps more on demure, shy women who are generally faithful than on others. Directness, liveliness, brazenness, etc., are always successful in love and as necessary as they are effective with more or less any kind of woman, since this is almost the only way to win them. But when considered simply as a means of pleasing and making a big impression on first meeting, there's no doubt that these qualities are more effective with demure, withdrawn, fearful women who have no experience of love affairs, etc., than with the other kind.

Vice versa, a serious, reserved man, or one who is modest, friendly, with no particular pretensions or boldness, the kind who doesn't throw himself determinedly at a woman, either because he doesn't know how to, doesn't dare, or doesn't want to, the withdrawn kind of man, etc., will make a much bigger impression on women who are loose and up front, women used to flirtations and flattery, etc., than on women of his own temperament. On the contrary, they'll dislike him from the start, or soon get bored, whereas the bolder kind will respond in the opposite way. Even men who are awkward and shy, etc., who lack the self-assurance and experience to be good conversationalists or approach women, with maybe a certain ingenuous air about them, of simplicity and innocence (the opposite of slyness), an air of *naturalness*, etc., are perfectly capable of completely turning off women who are like themselves, while on the other hand attracting the attention of women who are all too uninhibited, worldly wise, sly and free in their behavior and decisions, and up to every trick and maneuver people are in the habit of using; to such women these men will seem charming, etc.

Philosophical Thoughts—Consolation— Stubbornness—Memories of My Life

Mediocre spirits are always easily persuaded to believe in things or to do things and in one way or another will fall into line with a man of talent, or a con man, or anyone who for whatever reason has power over them or knows how to get it. Stubbornness in one's own views on the contrary is typical of both great and small spirits, or spirits more or less inferior or superior to mediocrity, but to the greater more than the smaller. The same goes for the susceptibility to being consoled. Just that here great spirits are less susceptible to consolation than small, because the truth, which they well understand, is never a source of consolation, and because the person trying to console won't easily be able to deceive them, which is the only way to console anyone.

Man Gets Used to Anything—The Ancients—Youth— Inaction—Man's Inclinations—Boredom—Handbook of Practical Philosophy—Memories of My Life

Man gets used to anything, but never to doing nothing. Time that softens all things, saps and destroys, never destroys or saps the disgust and *weariness* man feels in doing nothing. Long habit can have an effect on inaction, in that it can shift action from the outer life to the inner, so that a man prevented from moving, or from taking action in the outer world, will little by little develop the habit of becoming active within, of keeping himself company, in short of thinking, imagining, and entertaining himself intensely with his thoughts alone (as children do, or prisoners get used to doing). But pure boredom, pure emptiness, will always be intolerable, and neither time nor any possible force (except those that numb, extinguish, or suspend the human faculties, like sleep, opium, torpor, total prostration of all strength, etc.) can serve to alleviate it. Every moment of pure inaction is as wearisome for a man after ten years of the same as it was the first time. Emptiness, doing nothing, not living, death, this is the only thing man is incapable of and will never get used to. Because man, living creatures in general, in fact everything that exists, is / are born to act, and to act as intensely as possible; by which I mean that man is born to action in the outer world, which is far more intense than action in the mind. All the more so because inner mental action damages the body, and damages it the more the greater and more insistent it is, while outer action has the opposite effect. As for the inner action of the imagination, it impatiently spurs us to outer action and demands it, and will reduce man to a violent state if it is denied. This is what young people and primitives crave for, likewise the ancients, and they can't be denied it without putting their natures in a violent state. This for no other reason than because man and all living creatures always and naturally tend toward life, and to that surplus of life congenial to them.

Indecision — Reflection. Lack of Reflection — Reflective Men — Handbook of Practical Philosophy — Memories of My Life

The reflective man very often needs to be pushed to decide by the man who, whether by nature or out of habit, or in response to pressing circumstances, etc., doesn't reflect. He needs advice more than others, not because he can't see things well enough himself, but because he sees too much, which is precisely what leads to his interminable and pathetic indecision.

Man's Inclinations—Pleasure, Theory of—
Handbook of Practical Philosophy.

Doing something energetic, or using energy, whether passively or actively (taking a brisk walk, for example, or making powerful, vigorous movements, etc.), when and so far as this doesn't exceed an individual's strength, is a pleasure in itself, even when it may be uncomfortable (exposing oneself to intense cold, etc.) and even when there is no one to watch, and quite apart from any ambition or inner satisfaction and complacency one might also feel as a result. And it's not just doing energetic things; seeing them done is also a pleasure; watching active, energetic, rapid goings-on, movements, etc., that are lively, strong, difficult, etc., etc., actions, and so on, pleases us because it puts the mind into a kind of action and communicates a certain inner activity to it, *shakes it up*, etc., exercises it at a distance, etc., and the mind seems to come away from the experience stronger and exercised.

I've said before that every feeling of physical energy is a pleasure. The same is true in the mind (actually, every time our spirits are roused by some outer feeling of whatever kind, whether through reading, or some spectacle, or speech, or thinking, it's always a pleasure); the same goes for every act drawing on spiritual energy, like virtuous or energetic decisions, sacrifices, giving things up, etc., etc.

In short, a living creature of its essence tends toward life. Life is a pleasure for him, and likewise everything that is lively, even when it comes in the form of death. Man's happiness consists in the liveliness of his feelings and life, which is why he loves life. And this liveliness is never so great as when it is physical. The natural state provided wonderfully well for this *basic* and *universal* human inclination.

Moral Duties

I've said elsewhere that nature seems to have entrusted to each and every individual the preservation and care of order, reason, justice, existence, etc., as far as regards other individuals and all other beings; in short, it seems that each individual has been charged with the preservation of the whole of nature and all its laws, even where and when these have nothing at all to do with us. Hence our anger when we hear about some crime, a murder, for example, of someone we know nothing about, someone remote from any relationship with us however slight, any shared cause, and even when the murderer is likewise completely unknown to us. We immediately feel—the more so if we have a lively imagination and warm feelings, less if we are corrupt and perverted by cold reason—an intense hatred toward the criminal, a desire for revenge, almost as if we ourselves were the victims, and again an intense pleasure if we hear that this criminal has fallen into the hands of the law, disappointment if he escapes. This is especially true when for whatever reason we find the account of the crime compelling, and far more so when the crime takes place in our presence, etc. A man with abundant energy will feel the desire to avenge the crime himself, even when it has nothing to do with him and doesn't affect him in any way at all. This is why whenever news gets around of some particularly ugly crime people are always extremely happy when the criminal is captured, they look forward to it, applaud it, and during the trial they talk about his eventual punishment as of some plea-sure and gratification they're looking forward to, hoping on, and they complain about the judges being so slow, and if the accused is acquitted, they're upset, as if they personally had been offended. If he's declared guilty they're delighted, until anger over the crime gives way to compassion for the punishment.

On the other hand, compassion for the victim of the crime hardly has any part in the basic cause of all this reaction; on the con-trary, such compassion is very often and for various reasons, either insignificant or nonexistent, and anyhow in no way proportionate to the reactions described above; then there are crimes that have no particular victim yet outrage the public just the same.

What's more, although they appear entirely natural, innate, and elementary, all this reaction, all these feelings, actually derive from habit and what people are used to. At least up to a certain point, since, as I've said elsewhere, I believe that a nonpredatory animal *naturally* hates a carnivorous animal, when it sees it claw, kill, and devour its prey, even though in reality it isn't transgress-ing any law of its own nature, but very much transgresses the laws nature has laid down for noncarnivorous animals. Thus justice and our sense of good and evil, right and wrong, are merely relative, and don't depend on any *preceding* model or reasoning at all, etc., etc., etc.

Habit—Man's Inclinations—Memory—Of Nature

Anyone eager to confirm that human faculties are all acquired, and to see the difference between what is acquired and what is natural or innate, should watch how all the faculties that man is capable of are far stronger in the mature (and cultured, etc.) man than in the child, though the child is by no means absolutely without faculties, and how they grow together with the person: inclinations on the other hand, which are innate and generally speaking, as I have pointed out here and there of this or that inclination and as one could well say of all of them (so long as they are natural and not themselves acquired), unlike faculties, are stronger, livelier, more remarkable and numerous, etc., the closer a man is to the natural state, which is to say in the child, or primitive man, or savage, or uneducated man, etc. And though the human faculties grow stronger with time, both in an individual and in peoples or in the world, nevertheless, since a person (everyone or just someone) can be disposed to a faculty in two ways, one acquired, and the other natural and innate, the acquired elements will grow stronger in the same way as the faculties as a whole do, while the innate elements, being natural qualities, are much stronger in natural man, and particularly in children, than in the civilized man or the adult, so that one sees every day how children are able to assimilate and learn, etc., things that grown men can't, if they didn't start as children. In short, everything natural is stronger and more evident the less cultivated a person is, etc., and everything that gets stronger with cultivation is not natural, etc., etc.

Compassion — Desperation — Youth — Resignation — Sensitivity. Feeling — Sensitive People — Memories of My Life

I've said that people of great feeling are liable to become insensitive sooner and more markedly than others, especially those whose sensitivity is mediocre. This truth can be extended and applied to all those areas and forms, etc., in which feeling manifests itself and operates, like compassion, etc., etc. Although it's true that the man of feeling is destined to be unhappy, all the same it frequently happens that as a young man he becomes insensitive to grief and trouble, and that the less susceptible he now is, having gone beyond a certain age and been through a certain mill of experience, to intense grief, so all the more violent and terrible was his grief and desperation in his early years and tribulations. He often arrives quite young at a point where even an intense unhappiness can't seriously upset him, having passed swiftly from an excessive susceptibility to being excessively distressed, to the opposite, an attitude of calm and resignation so constant and so insensitive in its desperation that a new trouble will have no effect on him (and this one might describe as the last stage of feeling, one where the greatest natural disposition to imagination and feeling becomes almost entirely useless, and the greatest poet, the most eloquent imaginable, loses these qualities almost completely and irreversibly and becomes quite incapable of exploring them further or using them in whatever circumstances. Feeling is always intense up to this point, even in the midst of the greatest desperation and the most powerful awareness of the meaninglessness of everything. But after this, things become so empty to the sensitive man that he no longer senses even their emptiness: and at this point feeling and the imagination are truly dead, and beyond rescue). Nothing violent can last. People of mediocre feeling, on the other hand, will remain more or less susceptible to intense unhappiness their whole lives and always capable of new sorrows, in old age hardly less than in youth, as one sees every day in ordinary folk.

Self-Regard—Pleasure, Theory of

Not only do egoism and self-regard turn up in whatever act or sentiment man can possibly engage in, even those that seem at the farthest remove from self-regard and the most alien to it, but in those same acts and sentiments that seem distant from it, it plays just as large a part and is present in just as great a degree and with the same force and in the same amount—the person, or indeed any other living being, investing just as much in himself or itself—as in those acts and sentiments that derive from the purest, most straightforward, disgraceful and manifest selfishness.

This is important. Not only is man or any living being incapable of shaking off self-regard, but he can't shake it off even for a tiny part of his life (however much the very different forms this passion takes might lead us to suppose the contrary). And not only can self-regard not fade away altogether, it can't even fade the tiniest bit, ever; so you can say of it what they say of matter, that it has never increased nor decreased at all, there's exactly the same amount around today as there was at the beginning of the world and always will be. Because just as self-regard can't diminish, so it can't increase either, not in any individual, from the beginning of life to the end. (*Another demonstration and analogous observation proving that and in what way self-regard is infinite.*)

As a result self-regard is always present in the same amount in each and every moment of our lives; as much in the man who betrays his most sacred duties and principles to grab himself some small pleasure, as in the man who acts and performs the most heroic and terrible sacrifice so as to observe the smallest duty, or in the man who takes his own life.

What's more, the quantity of self-regard is exactly the same in every living creature of whatever species, *because it is infinite, and hence can be neither less nor more in any individual, either with respect to its own stability over time, or comparatively with any other individual whatever.*

The which, putting it the other way round, demonstrates, as I said, that it is *infinite, absolutely and in itself.*

Supreme Egoism of Fear—Fear

Fear is the direct child of self-regard and self-preservation, and hence inseparable from man, but most of all manifest in and proper to primitive man, children, and those who are closest to the natural state; it's a passion that man holds most intimately in common with every animal species and a general characteristic of living creatures; as a passion it is the most selfish there is. A fearful man withdraws into perfect isolation, cuts himself off from his nearest and dearest and hardly thinks twice about sacrificing them, etc., to save himself (on the contrary, it's as if he's disposed to do so by natural necessity). And when he's afraid a man doesn't cut himself off just from others, or from everything that in some way belongs to others, but from his own belongings as well, the things closest, most precious, and most necessary to him, like the sailor who dumps the fruits of years of hard work into the sea, of his entire life even, the very means of his subsistence. Hence we can say that fear is the perfection and the purest quintessence of egoism, because it reduces man not only to taking care only of his own things, but to letting even those go so as to take care exclusively of his own pure and naked self, the barest existence of his own individual life, cut off from every other possible existence. Man will even sacrifice parts of himself when he fears for his life, all his care and passion being reduced, cowed by fear, to concentrating on survival and exclusively on what is absolutely necessary for survival at any given moment. One might say that his very self shrinks and contracts the better to survive, allowing him to jettison any part of himself not strictly necessary, to save only what is inseparable from his being, only what makes it up, the essential part in which it necessarily and substantially consists.

Desperation — Pleasure of Desperation — Memories of My Life

DIDO, AENEID 4, 659 FF.

Moriemur inultae, Sed moriamur, ait. Sic sic iuvat ire sub umbras. [I shall die unavenged, but let me die — she says — like this, like this it's good to go down among the shades.]

Here Virgil wanted to get across (and it's a deep, subtle sentiment, worthy of a man who knew the human heart and had experience of passion and tragedy) the pleasure the mind takes in dwelling on its downfall, its adversities, then picturing them for itself, not just intensely, but minutely, intimately, completely; in exaggerating them even, if it can (and if it can, it certainly will), in recognizing, or imagining, but definitely in persuading itself and making absolutely sure it persuades itself, beyond any doubt, that these adversities are extreme, endless, boundless, irremediable, unstoppable, beyond any redress, or any possible consolation, bereft of any circumstance that might lighten them; in short in seeing and intensely feeling that its own personal tragedy is truly immense and perfect and as complete as it could be in all its parts, and that every door toward hope and consolation of any kind has been shut off and locked tight, so that now he is quite alone with his tragedy, all of it. These are feelings that come in moments of intense desperation as one savors the fleeting comfort of tears (when you take pleasure supposing yourself as unhappy as you can ever be), sometimes even at the first moment, the first emotion, on hearing the news, etc., that spells disaster, etc.

Sorrow—Memories of My Life

Every man of feeling will experience sorrow, or feel moved and melancholy, when he turns his thoughts to something that is finished forever, especially if in its time this thing was part of his life. I'm talking about anything liable to end, like a person's life or company, even a person you didn't particularly care for (even someone irksome and hateful), or this person's youth; a custom, a way of life, etc. Except in cases where this thing now over forever was actually painful, a misfortune, etc., or some drudgery, or where its being over is the result of it having reached its objective, achieved the end it set itself, etc. Although even here, if we had grown used to the thing, we still feel, etc. The only thing we're never unhappy to see the back of is boredom. The reason for these sentiments lies in that *infinite* that the idea of something that is *over* contains within itself, I mean beyond which there is *nothing*; of something over *forever*, that will *never* come back.*

>   *Everything that is over, every last time, always and *naturally* provokes sorrow and sadness. At the same time it excites a pleasant feeling, pleasant in this very same sorrow, this because of the infiniteness of the idea contained within those words, *finished*, *last*, etc. (which of their nature are and always will be extremely poetic, however common and ordinarily used they may be *in whatever language and style*. And so, again *in whatever language*, etc., are the other words and ideas I've noted in various entries as being poetic in themselves and because of the infiniteness that in essence they contain).

Self-Regard — Illusions — Hope — Memories of My Life

The human mind is always deceived in its hopes, and always open to deception: always misled by hope itself and always open to being misled: not just open to hope but possessed by it even in the moment of its final desperation, even in the act of suicide. Hope is like self-regard, from which it directly derives. Neither the one nor the other, for the very nature and essence of the animal we are, can ever abandon us as long as we live, for as long, that is, as we feel our existence.

Unlikely Today—The Ancients—Grief—Joy—
Passions of the Ancients—Memories of My Life—
Theory of the Arts. Practical Part

That the passions of the ancients were incomparably more
intense than those of the moderns, their effects far louder, more
dramatic, more real, and more furious, and that when expressing
them one ought to use far stronger lines and colors that one does
for modern passions, these are things that have been said over and
over again. But I think we need to draw attention to an important
difference between the various passions and, comparatively, their
greater or lesser intensity among the ancients and the moderns; and
to include all of them in two general categories I'm going to take as
certain (as everyone does) that the grief of the ancients was far more
intense and energetic, more openly expressed, more frantic and terrible (albeit, and perhaps for the same reasons, briefer) than that of
the moderns. But when it comes to joy, I'm not so sure, and I tend
to think that, at least in many cases, this passion may be more furious and violent among the moderns than the ancients, and this for
no other reason than because today this passion is rarer and briefer
than ever, just as grief was in ancient times. This observation could
be useful to dramatists, painters, and other artists representing the
passions. It's true that in children joy and grief are both more violent and for the same reason briefer than in adults. And it's also true
that the modern mindset encourages people to contain any strong
impression or affection they have and reflect it inwardly onto the
spirit, not letting it out at all, or hardly, and not allowing it to affect
things outside themselves. All the same I think that my observa-

tion above could be of some pertinence, particularly with regard to people who are not very, or not entirely, trained and disciplined in polite society or in the doctrines and science of things and man; and likewise those whose experience and habits of life, society, and human affairs hasn't induced them to conform to the norm, or drilled them into that apathy and coldness toward themselves and everything else that characterizes our century.

Communicating Pleasures to Others—
Secrets—Loneliness—Memories of My Life

That some people find it hard to keep a secret is something that can be attributed at least in part to that inclination people have to share their joys and troubles with others and tell them of any unusual feelings they may have, a tendency I've noted and explained elsewhere on various occasions. Usually we think of women and children as having problems keeping secrets, but this fault is also typical of anyone who whether by nature or by habit finds it hard to resist, overcome, and repress his inclinations. All too often even men who are cautious and trained to keep control of themselves still find it hard to keep secrets, and whenever they are confiding in someone else or simply talking, discussing, or chatting, they feel an inner urge to tell (even when this would be damaging to them). The same is true even when it's not someone else's secret that's at stake but our own, and when we're aware that revealing it would damage only or mainly ourselves, which was precisely why we had decided not to talk about it, and then we go and tell anyway because we can't keep our big mouths shut.

Anger—Memories of My Life

When it comes, for example, to anger or impatience over one's troubles, don't we find that this passion is extremely varied and changeable not only from one species to another, one individual to another, but even in the same individual, depending on the circumstances? Put a man in trouble and let him get used to it. However impatient by nature, with time he'll become inured to it and extremely patient. (I can testify personally to every part of this proposition.) Imagine that this same man has never suffered at all, or let him get used to things going well again, or imagine another individual in one of these two circumstances, even someone extremely calm by nature. Every upset, however slight, will make him impatient. Now what could be a more fundamental consequence of self-regard than this impatience with any trouble that befalls a self in love with itself? Yet this impatience is greater or smaller depending on temperament, species, and character, and then varies in the same individual according to circumstances and habits. Likewise the self-regard that produces it.

Fate

Even today, with superstition all but stamped out everywhere, horror and fear of fate and destiny are still felt more by strong and great minds than by mediocre ones, this because the strong-minded have clear aims and ambitions that they pursue with unflagging energy and steady determination. This was more ordinarily the case in ancient times, when tenacity, constancy, strength, and generosity were commoner virtues than in modern times. And seeing that very often, all too frequently, in fact, life's circumstances set themselves against men's wishes, they were overcome by fear because they couldn't stop wanting their goal and planning their every action toward something that they realized might not, and actually very probably would not, ever be achieved. In fact, given the infinite variety of chance, it's far less likely that the thing you're working toward so determinedly will happen, rather than one of the infinite other possibilities. Now, if one of those other outcomes does occur, this is the effect not of a fixed destiny that's persecuting you, but of blind accident. These men, however, as is natural and as though in response to an optical or mechanical illusion, confused (and strong impassioned minds still do confuse) their own intransigence in desiring their goal with that of the unfolding events, and since they weren't the kind of people to run with the tide or adapt, they imagined the intransigence lay not in themselves but in a series of events predetermined by destiny. Mediocre spirits, on the other hand, lacking determination or steady ambitions, but having any number of goals, either allow chance to choose one or more of these for them without much resistance, or, even when that's not the case, yield to the course of events without a struggle, allowing themselves to be shifted, buckled, and directed in line with how things go. Having no fixed point in themselves, and seeing no supreme difficulty in reconciling their own plans to events as they happen, their minds are freer and they don't suppose that fortune is opposing them with a strong and steady counterforce (the which strength and steadiness is actually nothing other than the resistance great minds oppose to extremely unstable, random events), but take everything as the result of chance and coincidence, which in fact it is. Let's add to this the steadfastness, in noble minds, with regard not only to the goals pursued but also to the means adopted, a steadfastness that doesn't allow them to change their principles, or adapt their behavior to events, but keeps them ever constant in their goals and in their methods of achieving those goals, while the opposite happens with lesser men. And even in the absence of any particular plan or goal, a firm unchanging character will experience the illusion of an opposing force of destiny, the course of events being so various as to seem unyielding to someone who sees only one way forward, only one manner of behaving, thinking, doing, only one kind of thing that should happen, and how it should happen, or how they feel it should. And to a greater or lesser degree you find this fear of destiny in mediocre minds too, or entirely reasonable, philosophical, etc., minds, when they do have some desire or do aim at some goal in such a way as to become intransigent with regard to that point. See Staël, *Corinne*, bk. 13, ch. 4, p. 306, tome 2, edition cited above. This illusion I've been talking about you could compare in a way to our false impression when we imagine the earth is motionless because we are standing still on it, when in fact it is spinning and whirling at great speed. And already one can see that even in noble minds this illusion is more intense and present when they are going through periods of intense desires and determined, impetuous, strong, steady ambitions, etc., great passions, etc.

Ancients—Heroes. Heroism—Fate

Ses héros aiment mieux être écrasés par la foudre que de faire une bassesse, ET LEUR COURAGE EST PLUS INFLEXIBLE

QUE LA LOI FATALE DE LA NÉCESSITÉ. [His heroes would rather be struck by lightning than do anything base, AND THEIR COURAGE IS MORE INFLEXIBLE THAN THE FATAL LAW OF NECESSITY.] Barthélemy on Aeschylus.

Ancients—Consolation—Fate—Necessity— Suicide—Memories of My Life

A great mind does not yield to necessity; on the contrary, there is nothing, perhaps, that leads such a person to nurture an atrocious, declared, and savage hatred of himself and of life as the thought that his troubles, misery, calamities, etc., are inevitable and irreversible. Only a mean, or weak, or vacillating person, or someone who has no strength of passion, by nature perhaps, or through habit, or as a result of dealing over the years with all kinds of bad luck, hardships, and experience of things and of the way the world is, hardships that have subdued and tamed him—only people like this bend to necessity and actually take comfort from it amid their troubles, saying it would have been crazy to resist and fight them, etc. But the ancients, greater, nobler, and stronger than us as they always were, finding themselves overwhelmed by events, and thinking on their inevitability, the invincible power of the forces that made them wretched and that fastened and bound them to their wretchedness so that it was impossible to turn things round or escape, nurtured a hatred and fury against fate and cursed the Gods, declared war almost against the heavens, powerless though they were and with no hope of victory or revenge, but still not subdued or tamed, or any less determined to take their revenge, quite the contrary in fact, more determined than ever the greater the wretchedness and the more it was inevitable. There are plenty of examples of this in the stories we have. What the dying Julian is supposed to have done may just be fable, I don't know. Niobe, if I'm not mistaken, cursed the Gods after her catastrophe and declared herself beaten but still unyielding. We who don't believe in fortune or destiny, and don't recognize any personification of the necessity that forces events on us, have no one we can turn our hatred and fury against (even if we are noble and constant and unyielding by nature), no one but ourselves, that is; and hence we nurture against our own person a truly lethal hatred, as if we were our own most bitter and primary enemies, and we cheer ourselves with thoughts of suicide and self-mutilation, taking pleasure in the misery that oppresses us, and we come to wish that it was even greater, as when someone plans revenge against an object of supreme anger and hatred. For myself, every time I have been convinced of the inevitability and permanence of my misery, every time, looking desperately, frenetically, this way and that, I have been bound to realize that there is no possible remedy, no hope at all; instead of yielding, or consoling myself with the reflection that the situation was impossible and the result of forces beyond my control, I found myself nurturing a furious hatred against myself, because the misery I hated was located nowhere but in myself; so I was the only possible object of my hatred, since I had no one else, recognized no one else whom I could blame for my troubles and no one else who could become a target of my hatred for this reason. I conceived a burning desire to take revenge on myself and on my own life for a misery that was inevitable and inseparable from my very being and I experienced a fierce joy, a supreme joy, at the thought of suicide. The unyielding world clashed with my own unyielding nature and when the collision came—me incapable of giving way, easing off, or backing down and the world even less so—the loser in the struggle could only be me. Today (except when our ills depend on other people) we don't see anyone to blame for our misery, or anyone whom Religion doesn't do everything to prevent us from thinking of as to blame, and hence a proper object of our hatred. All the same, even in the Religion we have today, when misery goes beyond the norm and is not dependent on other people, or visible entities, sometimes someone will develop a hatred against superior and invisible entities and curse them; and this the more so the more that person (steadfast and noble in spirit) is religious and a believer. Job turned to moaning and almost cursing as much God as himself and his own life, his own birth, etc.

Satirical Thoughts—Upbringing. Teaching—Fate—Fortune. Fortune's Tricks—Those Who Govern—Mythologies—Memories of My Life

People governed by others in public or in private life—and the more strictly governed they are (as is the case with children and youngsters) the more true this will be—always accuse, or naturally tend to accuse, those who govern them of being responsible for their ills, or for their not having all the things they'd like to have, and likewise for whatever bothers and frustrates them, this even in areas where it's perfectly obvious that those doing the governing are not responsible and not in a position to prevent or alleviate those ills or procure the things wanted, having nothing whatsoever to do with either, there being no relation between the two. The reason for this is that since man is always unhappy he naturally tends, again without exception, to blame his unhappiness not on the nature of things and people (and much less to refrain from blaming anyone), but always to blame someone or something in particular, someone on whom he can vent the bitterness that his sufferings have caused and who will serve as an object for his hatred and protests, protests he would enjoy a great deal less if they were not directed against someone he feels is to blame for his suffering. This natural tendency is such that the sufferer actually persuades himself of the truth of what he has imagined, and almost wishes things really were that way. That is how it came about that man imagined the names and personifications of fortune and fate, who for so long were blamed for human ills, and so sincerely hated by the ancients in their unhappiness, and against whom even today, when no other culprits present themselves, we turn in all seriousness our hatred and protest for whatever has gone wrong. But for both ancients and moderns it has always been far more satisfying to blame something visible, and best of all some other person, not just because they are more plausibly to blame, with the result that it's easier to convince ourselves that it's their fault, something important for us, but even more so because hatred and grumbling are more satisfying when directed against people really there, people who can witness our anger and be made subject to the vendetta we intend to wage against them with our empty hatred and empty protest. Then hatred and protesting are sweetest of all when turned against people like ourselves, this for various reasons, one of which is that only an intelligent being can really be considered to blame for anything. Those who govern us are easy choices when we're looking for someone to make responsible for ills that can't easily be attributed to anyone else, someone to serve as object and target for our vain craving for revenge, which seems to us to be a satisfying response to those same ills. In such cases these people are best suited to our purpose, the people we can most plausibly complain about to others and to ourselves. So it is that whoever governs, publicly or privately, is always an object of the hatred and grumbling of those they govern. *Men are always dissatisfied because they are always unhappy.* That's why they are dissatisfied with their condition, and for the same reason with those governing them. (They feel they are unhappy, they know very well how much they suffer, how little they enjoy things, and in this they are not deceived. They think they have a right to be happy and to enjoy life and not to suffer, and in this too they would hardly be in the wrong were it not for the fact that what they are asking for is, if nothing else, impossible.) And just as one can never arrange for men to be happy, or even satisfied, so no governor, public or private, however much he may love his subjects, however carefully he looks after them, however great his concern to deliver them from their ills and give them some relief — in short, however deserving he may be in their regard — can ever reasonably hope that they won't hate him and protest against him, the wisest included, because it is man's nature to moan about someone, almost as much as it is his nature to be unhappy, and this someone, ordinarily and very naturally, is the person governing him. So, sadly, when it comes to governing others there are only two truly wise positions to take: either you abstain from governing, publicly or privately, or you govern entirely for your own advantage and not for that of the people you're governing.

Love of One's Country—Love of One's Hometown— Greeks—Isocrates—Italy—City and Province— Provincial (Spirit)—Memories of My Life

Isocrates, in his *Panegyric*, p. 133, just before the middle, when he starts to talk about the two Persian wars, praising the customs and institutions of those who ruled Athens and Sparta before the time of these wars, says: ἴδια μὲν ἄστη τὰς ἑαυτῶν πόλεις ἡγούμενοι, κοινὴν δὲ πατρίδα τὴν Ἑλλάδα νομίζοντες εἶναι. [They thought of their own States as their private homes, but considered Greece a common homeland.]

Compassion—Isocrates—Hardships

Isocrates, in his *Panegyric*, p. 150, just after the halfway point, reporting the harm done to their city by the supporters of the Spartans, says of them: εἰς τοῦτο δ' ὠμότητος ἅπαντας ἡμᾶς κατέστησαν, ὥστε πρὸ τοῦ μὲν διὰ τὴν παροῦσαν εὐδαμονίαν, κἂν ταῖς μικραῖς ἀτυχίαις, πολλοὺς ἕκαστος ἡμῶν εἶχε τοὺς συμπαθήσοντας · ἐπὶ δὲ τῆς τούτων ἀρχῆς, διὰ τὸ πλῆθος τῶν οἰκείων κακῶν, ἐπαυσάμεθα ἀλλήλους ἐλεοῦντες. Οὐδενὶ γὰρ τοσαύτην σχολὴν παρέλιπον, ὥσθ' ἑτέρῳ συναχθεσθῆναι. [They drove us to such levels of cruelty that whereas before, thanks to our prosperity, anyone who had even the most minor kind of trouble would find plenty of people who sympathized (he is speaking of private people, that is, each citizen individually), under their government we had so many personal hardships that we stopped pitying each other because our troubles left us no time to share in other people's grief.] It really is habitual suffering that makes man cruel, or ὠμὸν, as Isocrates said.*

> *I've said elsewhere that fear is the most selfish of the passions. Hence something often observed, that in times of plague or general calamity, when everyone fears for himself, the perils and deaths of our nearest and dearest produce no, or almost no, emotional effect on us.

What Arouses Love in the Old — Courage — Youth — The Old — Life — Memories of My Life

Love of life grows almost like love of money, and both increase to the extent that they ought to decline. That's why young people spurn life and squander it when it is sweet and when they have so much before them; and they're not afraid of death: and why old people fear death above all things and are extremely protective of their lives, however wretched they are, and however little they have left to preserve. And so the young man throws away what he has, as if he had only a few days to live, and the old man piles his things up, hoards, and saves, as if he had a long, long life stretching ahead to provide for.

Philosophical Thoughts—Courage—
Paradoxes—Fright—Fear

Fear is one thing and terror quite another. Terror is a much stronger and more intense feeling than fear, making it far more likely that your spirits will be depressed and reason suspended, in fact, that all your mental faculties and even physical sensations will be impaired. All the same, while fear doesn't occur in men who are wholly courageous and wise, terror does. Such men may never be afraid, but they can always be terrified. No one can rightly claim that he can't be frightened.

Self-Regard—Compassion—Egoism—Memories of My Life

One typical characteristic of man is that while another person's superiority, or virtue combined with success, will provoke only a mild interest in him—I mean admiration—another's suffering always rouses intense, lasting, and extremely pleasurable interest, and all the more so when the sufferer is virtuous. So it is that man takes pleasure in feelings of compassion through which, at no cost to himself, he achieves that feeling, so wonderfully gratifying in every situation and occasion—I mean a vague consciousness of his heroism and noble-heartedness. In nature adversity is a cause for contempt and even hatred toward the sufferer, since by nature man hates painful ideas the same way he hates pain itself. So by focusing on a sufferer's virtue, regardless of his calamity, not loathing or spurning him despite his being a victim, to the point finally of feeling compassion for him—I mean seeking to participate mentally in his troubles—we feel we are making an effort in spite of ourselves, overcoming our own nature, proving our nobleness and generosity, establishing a reason for persuading ourselves that we were born with a spirit superior to the ordinary man's; all the more so because since egoism is natural to man, by taking an interest in others, an interest that doesn't cost him anything, the compassionate man reckons he has shown how extraordinarily generous he is, how special, heroic, more than a man even, because capable of not being self-centered, and of involving himself, his very self, on behalf of others, others than himself. See pp. 3291–3297[*] and 3480–3482.[†] Taking pity, a man swells with pride and feels pleased with himself: so it is that he enjoys feeling pity, and is pleased with his compassion and with himself. The act of compassion is an act of pride that man accomplishes within himself. So compassion too, which you would have thought was the feeling farthest removed from self-regard, absolutely contrary to it in fact, and in no way or part reducible to self-regard or related to it, actually in substance (like all other feelings) turns out to derive precisely from self-regard, in fact is nothing but self-regard and an act of egoism. The which manages to produce and concoct a pleasure by imagining that it — egoism — has died, or at least suspended its normal operations, by turning the interest of the individual toward another person. So our egoism is gratified because it imagines it has stopped or suspended its very being egoistic. See p. 3167.[‡]

[*]We must distinguish between egoism and self-regard. The first is nothing more than a variety of the second. Egoism is when a man employs his self-regard in such a way as to think only of himself, not to do anything that is not immediately for himself, re-

jecting the idea of acting on behalf of others, with the long-range intention, hardly clear to the mind of the person acting, but extremely real, steady, and constant in practical terms, of directing all his activity toward himself as his ultimate and one true goal, something self-regard can and does do very well. I've said elsewhere that self-regard is stronger in the man who is more alive and has greater vitality and again that this greater vitality will be in proportion to a greater strength and activity of mind and indeed of body. But while this could not be more true of self-regard, it is not and shouldn't be understood as being so of egoism. Otherwise old people, modern man, men with little feeling and imagination would be less egoistic than children and young people, the ancients, sensitive men, and people with powerful imaginations. Whereas this is precisely the opposite of the case. But not when it comes to self-regard. Because self-regard is indeed much stronger in children and young people than in adults and old people, stronger in sensitive and imaginative people than in dull. (That self-regard is greater in children and young people than in older people is evident from that infinite and extremely sensitive tenderness they have toward themselves, and likewise that susceptibility and sensitivity and delicacy they have with regard to their own person, a quality that falls off in proportion to increasing age and experience until in the end it tends to be lost.) Children, young people, sensitive people are far more tender toward themselves than are their counterparts. The same could be said of strong people with respect to weak. So generally speaking were the ancients with respect to the moderns, and natural man with respect to civilized man, since, being of strong constitution and stronger, more active and more vivacious in spirit and imagination (thanks to both physical and moral circumstances), they were less disillusioned, and simply more and more intensely alive. (From which it should follow that the ancients were generally more unhappy than the moderns, if we accept that unhappiness is in direct proportion to a greater self-regard, as I have demonstrated elsewhere: but since the ancients employed and applied their energies infinitely more than we do today, and enjoyed infinitely more distractions and the like, and since the greater intensity of outer life was more than in proportion to the greater intensity of inner life, the fact remains, as I have demonstrated over and over again, that the ancients were on the contrary a thousand times less unhappy than the moderns: and the same can be said of natural man and civilized man: but not of young people versus old people today, because young people today are denied a sufficient use of their energies, and engagement with the outer life, something that nowadays is enjoyed almost as much by the old as the young; as a result of which and for those other reasons I've spoken about in various places, today young people are unhappier than older people, a conclusion that, again, I have reached elsewhere.)

Since sacrifice of self and self-regard, whatever the nature of the sacrifice, can only (like every other human action) proceed from self-regard itself, and since such sacrifice is something extraordinary, above nature, and more than animal (certainly there are no examples of such a thing in any animal or being other than man), more than human in fact, it cannot occur without a very great, indeed extraordinary energy and abundance of self-regard. So it is that where self-regard is most abundant, where it has most energy, that is where self-sacrifice, compassion, and the habit of and inclination toward acts of charity will be greatest and most frequent. Thus it is that all this ought to be present and indeed is present and more frequent among young people, the ancients, sensitive people with lively minds, and finally men who, generally speaking, have a greater quantity and energy of self-regard and less egoism, than you find in adults and old people, the moderns (except in regard to compassion, as I've said in the places cited above, since there was very little the ancients would sacrifice themselves for, aside from their homeland), people who are dull and insensitive and hard-hearted, people of slow, dead minds, and finally women, since women usually have more egoism in terms of both quantity and energy and less self-regard.

Narrowing things down, my first conclusion is that, far from being in direct proportion to self-regard, egoism is actually inversely proportionate to it; egoism is a marker and a consequence either of a dearth and essential feebleness of self-regard, or of its decline and weakening; it generally abounds and is stronger in those centuries, peoples, sexes, individuals, and at those ages of the same individuals when life is less intense and hence self-regard in short supply, and colder and weaker.

My second conclusion is that old people and adults, the moderns, insensitive people, and women are more egoistic and display a lower level and intensity of self-regard than children and young people, the ancients, sensitive people, and men (because they have less life or vitality, and egoism is a dead quality, a dead passion, or as little alive as anything can be). (From these theories it follows that animals, having less life than man, since they have less spirit and more matter, a great proportion of themselves that exists without being alive, etc., must have less self-regard and more egoism; and so it is: and that among the animals the less vital species—the octopus, the snail, etc.—must be the more egoistic: and that descending to the vegetable world and thence through the whole chain of being, one can say that the less life there is, the stronger egoism becomes, so that the least organized of beings is in a certain sense the most egoistic, etc.) And that as a result these people—the old, the moderns, women, etc.—are naturally less willing and less likely to make sacrifices for anyone or anything, to show compassion whether actively or passively, to be charitable or generally to do things for others: all of which is evidently the case and can't be denied. (The same can be said with relation to the weak and the strong, people who are usually unfortunate and those usually fortunate, and the like; all qualities that correspond to, and from which will spring, a greater or lesser vitality, and a habit of being active and lively, which will be more intense in the strong and the fortunate and less so in the weak and the unfortunate.) (Likewise the climates and the seasons, insofar as they influence the level of life and vitality, inner or outer activity, etc., will also influence the level of self-regard and hence the level of egoism too, and the natural disposition toward compassion and benevolence, etc.)

However, one could make an exception in favor of women when it comes to compassion, especially the kind that doesn't lead to action. This is because compassion requires, as has been said before, not just greater vitality, and hence ever more intense self-regard, but also a greater refinement and delicacy of self-regard and spirit: and women perhaps are, or are certainly reputed to be, generally superior in these qualities, all other things being equal, to men. The same could be said of the moderns with respect to the ancients. In all those aspects of compassion or charity that require delicacy or greater delicacy, fineness of feeling, and almost an affectation of self-regard, a finesse, rather than vitality, energy, strength and abundance of self-regard, abundance and intensity of life; in all those aspects, and in everything that has to do with them, my point is that women, the moderns, and anyone who, like them, has developed these qualities of delicacy, will generally speaking surpass men, the ancients, natural man, the common peasant, and so on. This in line with what I said in the pages cited above.

Thus it is that insofar as they are weaker and needier, women are less compassionate and charitable than men; but insofar as they are more delicate in both mind and body, they will be more so. But I believe that the qualities of weakness and neediness will generally prevail and weigh more heavily and more obviously in the balance than delicacy and the like. Thus, overall, women really are, generally and because of their nature, more egoistic, and hence less compassionate (especially when it comes to compassion that actually does things) and less charitable than men. This because intensity, strength, and abundance of life, and hence of self-regard, play a much greater part in charity and in a readiness to sacrifice oneself, the act of sacrifice itself and the exclusion of egoism, than do delicacy and fineness of mind uncoupled from strength and energy and activity and the lively inner life of self-regard. And this not only in men as compared with women, but generally in anyone as compared with anyone else. (Following this line of argument, an old woman, especially one who has lived in high society, must by nature and generally speaking be the most egoistic human being imaginable.)

†I was observing a sickeningly egoistic old man, so pleased with himself as he spoke of some tiny sacrifices he had made, some small hardships he had accepted (true or false as the case might be, genuinely voluntary or otherwise), and he spoke with a certain bashfulness, making it perfectly clear, especially to anyone who knew the man's character, how convinced he was that he had behaved heroically, and that these sacrifices and hardships showed what a truly superior fellow he was, putting aside his own pleasures and self-regard. It was very important to him that others should think the same way—indeed, that was why he was talking about it—but he made it plain enough that this really was his own view of the matter. One notes here the power, even in a man absolutely rooted in egoism, quite blunt about it, intolerant of the slightest inconvenience and capable of sacrificing anyone and anything for his own slightest convenience, the power, as I was saying, in someone with a mind like this, a real loner, totally inert and absolutely

cut off from society, of this desire to seem to others, but to himself as well, capable of great sacrifices, superior to his own self-regard, the opposite of the egoist, and, in short, a hero. The fact is that there's almost no one so brazenly and absolutely egoistic in his behavior that he does not earnestly wish to appear, at least to himself, and who does not in fact persuade himself to be, and take enormous pleasure in thinking of himself as, a hero. Everyone loves building up his self-esteem, and you can be sure that everyone, one way or another, admires himself, admires himself greatly, in the same way they love themselves, I mean constantly, without a second's break; although self-esteem (like love, too, for that matter, as I have shown elsewhere) grows and falls off in the same individual depending on the circumstances and for various reasons. What I've said here about old people who are egoistic can equally be applied to children, who are extremely self-centered; unaware of heroism as yet, since no one has spoken to them about it, they nevertheless yearn for all kinds of small distinctions, like being ill or having others imagine they are ill, so as to grab attention in the family, or resembling the adults in some way, that's something they aspire to constantly, and across the board in thousands of little things, just out of vanity, or let's call it ambition, etc. See Alfieri's account of himself as a boy pretending to be a soldier on parade.

‡Another way an egoist puffs up his self-regard is by persuading himself that he is not egoistic, that he loves others aside from himself, and by imagining he has demonstrated this to himself. Hence for the refined mind compassion toward an enemy is even sweeter than compassion toward friends or people who are neither one nor the other, first because you can persuade yourself so much more easily and convincingly that the feeling you're experiencing is pure and absolutely uncontaminated by selfishness or influenced by it; and then because the greater the idea you dream up of the greatness, generosity, and nobility of your own mind,

the more you swell up in your own eyes (thinking about the compassion you're showing to your enemies, of all people), an effect of compassion that I have already spoken about. So in the *Iliad* Homer shows supreme art and exquisite intentions and purpose and achieves extraordinarily beautiful results when he sets out to make compassion one of the main emotions of his work, and then addresses that compassion, which animates the whole poem, mainly to his enemies.

Compassion

Just as respect for an enemy, albeit beaten and obedient, was not a characteristic of ancient times, neither was compassion for the enemy (see what I have said elsewhere with regard to Aeneas after the death of Pallas). In man's natural state, the only pleasure a person takes in victory is the pleasure of revenge. Compassion, even generally speaking (I mean the compassion for people who aren't our enemies), is, as I've said before, a product of our self-regard; it is a pleasure, but not one typical of animals or men in the natural state, nor even, except perhaps rarely and to a small degree, among people who are barely civilized (which was the situation at the times of the heroes). The pleasure of compassion can arise only where there is delicacy and ductility of emotion, or the emotional faculty, a refined and pliant self-regard that can bend like a snake to give its attention to others and convince itself that all its efforts are directed toward them, although in reality self-regard is still pulsing with life and working in itself and for itself, for the individual, that is, who is feeling the compassion. So it is that even in modern, civilized times compassion is typical only among cultured people and people who are by nature delicate and sensitive, which is to say re-

fined and lively. In the country, where it's true people are less corrupt than in the city, compassion is rare, not intimately or intensely
felt, ineffective and brief.

Compassion — Poetry of the Imagination

Returning to our main subject from this digression, which was
not, I think, without its relevance, it remains to reflect how strange,
almost absurd, it is that in the ferocious times he lived in Homer
put so much stress on compassion in his epic, made it a central,
indeed decisive source of interest, and that he carried through his
plan so well that even today, when other interest in *The Iliad* has
fallen away, there is still no other book perhaps that grips us more;
and that he didn't hesitate to direct that compassion, heightening
its intensity, almost entirely on the enemies of his compatriots, the
Greeks for whom he was writing, people who did not have a high
opinion of generosity toward their enemies but actually prized
the opposite qualities; and again that modern poets have deliberately excluded compassion as a principal interest in their work, and
for the most part have avoided directing it in any serious amount
toward the enemies of the heroes and peoples they have chosen to
praise (the compassion for Clorinda in *Jerusalem* wasn't a problem
because Tasso has her die as a convert and in the same canto reveals
that she had Christian parents and came from a Christian country;
so that in the end and in line with the poet's final intention, the
compassion is actually directed toward a Christian), etc., etc. The
exact opposite would have been more credible, and Tasso would
have done much better to have written it that way.

Upbringing. Teaching—Youth—Man's Aims—
Hope—Old Age—Memories of My Life

One can say of man's prospects, plans, resolutions, goals, hopes, and desires—in short, of everything in his thoughts that relates to the future—that the less time he naturally has to live the farther his plans will stretch into the distance and the more they will aim, point, or reach out toward the future, and vice versa. A newborn has no thoughts relating to the future, unless we think of the instant that follows immediately on the present moment as the future, since the present in fact is only an instant, and beyond that time is all and always either past or future. But if we think of present and future, not exactly and mathematically, but rather more generally, the way we usually imagine them and refer to them, then one has to admit that a baby thinks only of the present. And the child hardly projects much farther than that; with the result that proposing (e.g., in his studies) some distant goal to a child (like the glory and the benefits he might acquire in maturity or old age, or even in his youth), is absolutely pointless, won't motivate him at all (so that it's quite right and very effective to entice the child to study with the prospect of honors and rewards that can and should be achieved very soon, day by day almost, thus bringing the purpose of glory and the usefulness of study into his immediate field of vision, since otherwise he'll never set his eyes on those goals, while this approach helps him to get down to it and to put up willingly with the hard work and sacrifices that his nature loathes and that studying demands). The young man looks farther ahead, but nothing like as far as the mature and settled man whose calculations vis-à-vis the future, without his realizing it, very often go beyond a mortal man's natural span of life. Because the mature man is already beginning to take a huge pleasure in his hopes, to find happiness in those, even to live off them. Children and young people also feed on hopes, commune with them, and dream on them; but they're not content with just hoping; rather, they have to try to realize their hopes at once, put them into action, arrive at something concrete. This stems from the enthusiasm people have in their youth, mental activity fusing and conspiring with physical activity, the freshness and strength of their self-regard, and hence from the energy and practical thrust of desires that fret in the face of any delay and are unwilling to fasten on goals that can't be, or that they don't think can be, quickly and easily achieved; it also and finally stems from their inexperience when it comes to the vanity of human wishes, to the difficulties people have achieving their goals, and again to the emptiness of the things they hoped on, something that inevitably emerges the moment these things are possessed. The long-term, more remote outlook of the adult is explained by his having just the opposite qualities; and it is an excess of these opposite qualities in the old that results in an excess of the opposite attitude; that is, just when it would be unreasonable to suppose that they have more than a very brief period of life left to them, the old person's expectations extend far beyond those of adults and younger people. Weak now, physically and mentally, disillusioned with what wishes were fulfilled in the past, his self-regard on the wane in line with the waning and cooling of life, the old man is capable only of feeble desires, and hence is content to postpone their fulfillment to some distant future, slow them right down, so that the desires themselves are happy simply to hang on;

all too experienced in the vanity and disappointments of past hopes, he resorts to what is almost a trick, hoping on things so far away that there is no danger they'll disappear as he gets close to them or reaches them, or if this ever does happen it will only be very late in the day; to that we can add the lack of resolution typical of old age and the tendency to delay any action till later, qualities that oblige the older man to delay, defer almost, his hopes as well, likewise the objects of his desires and the moment when he plans to fulfill them, or to be more precise when he likes to dream of fulfilling them; and again there is his habit of doing things slowly, listlessly, something the feebleness and languor of old age forces on him, as well as the mental laziness, negligence, and torpor that are both results and causes of such laziness, so that his desires too and his hopes become tardy and lazy and slow, forgotten almost (though always just alive enough to support him, suckle him almost, something indispensable to human life), until he manages to convince himself, more with the imagination than the intellect, and through the unreasoning habit of his other mental faculties, that time and nature and the world have all slowed down, must slow down, until they are as slow and lazy as he is obliged to be.

Compassion — Charity — Education. Teaching — Memories of My Life

In my experience* and as one might explain the situation using reasons I've set out elsewhere, the habit of showing compassion and being charitable and doing things of whatever kind for others, and, where that isn't possible, the inclination to charity and to working on behalf of others, is always (leaving aside questions of character, temperament, upbringing, level of culture or coarseness, and suchlike) in direct relation to a person's strength and happiness, and to his not needing other people's assistance and generosity, or again in inverse proportion to his weakness and unhappiness, his experience of hardships and troubles, whether past or more especially present, and the need he has of other people's help and generosity. The more someone is in a position to be an object of compassion, or to yearn for it and demand it, and the more he does in fact yearn for it and demand it, even when he's in the wrong, and convince himself he deserves it, so the less he will show compassion himself, since he will now turn all his natural faculties and whatever habits of compassion he may once have had toward himself. The more a man needs the charity of others, so the less he himself is charitable, the less he is even inclined to charity; not only does he do less on behalf of others, but his enthusiasm for his own charitableness dwindles, even though this is the very quality he desires and expects in others, and that rightly or wrongly he supposes he deserves or needs. A weak man, one always needful of those greater or lesser acts of charity that people in society offer or receive and that are the main purpose for which society is formed, or at least the purpose that a reciprocating community should serve, is hardly or not at all inclined to do anything on behalf of others, and rarely or never actually does anything, and then only very little, even where he could do something, even for men weaker and needier than himself. Men inured to hardships, especially those for whom life is synonymous with suffering, a companion in misery, will not be moved, and certainly not moved to act, by the sight or thought of other people's trials, tribulations, and pains. When someone is unhappy, his self-regard is too busy with itself to allow him to pay attention to others. He has quite enough to do dealing with his own troubles; even if they are much smaller than those he sees in others. If he is going through troubles now, in the present, his compassion, as I said, is entirely turned toward himself, active on himself, so it's all used up and nothing is left over for anyone else. If his troubles are now past, the memory of them, however small they may have been, is such that he finds nothing extraordinary or specially terrible in the sufferings and disasters of others, nothing that would prompt him to do without his self-regard for a while and turn it to the benefit of others; as someone who knows about suffering, this person is content to offer tacit advice in his own mind to those in trouble, suggesting they resign themselves to their fate, and imagining he has the right to insist on this, as if he himself had already shown the way; because each after his fashion is convinced that he has borne or is bearing his troubles and pains in as manly a way as possible and with greater determination than others, or at least than most men in his position, would have done or would do; in the same way that each person thinks of himself as being less deserving than anyone else of the hardships he has faced or is facing. Add to which the fact that this attitude of insensitivity to other people's calamities, something one falls into when one has one's own troubles, is not easily thrown off, in part because it is so very much in line with one's self-regard, which is to say with man's very nature; and in part because hardship makes a profound and serious impression on a man, with the result that the effects it produces and leaves behind last a long time and may very often be decisive and permanent in forming a man's character for the rest of his life.

I've noticed (and I have more than one example in mind) that young people who aren't poor, or haven't been crushed or disheartened by poverty, people with healthy and hardy physiques, courageous and busy, capable of looking after themselves and with little or no need, or rather little or no desire, for help from others, or for the physical or moral support of others, at least not as a rule; young people still untouched by misfortune, or rather (since just being *born* means suffering), touched only in such a way that thanks to the energy of their youth and constitution and the freshness of their mental energies, they have been able to shrug it off on their own, and pay little attention to it; young people like this, as I was saying, although on the one hand they won't tolerate the slightest insult, have a tendency to lose their tempers and are more inclined than most to make fun of others, present or absent, and to be overbearing more often than not, both in the way they speak and even in the way they act, see pp. 3282[†] and 3942,[‡] and although again they may have been let down by everyone, perhaps by the very people whose most sacred duty it was to look after them, so that they are all too familiar with people's ingratitude and aware from experience of the lack of return or thanks resulting from being charitable, the damage rather that it may bring them; although also quick and shrewd of mind, not without a knowledge of the world, well aware that men are not customarily charitable or compassionate, far from it, on the contrary that their opinions actually lead them away from it, and then that most men are unworthy of other people's help; despite all this these young people are more than ready to show compassion, more than willing to come to the aid of those in trouble, more than well disposed to show charity and to help those who ask them for it, even if such folk are undeserving, and again to offer their help spontaneously, overcoming another's reluctance to accept it and unwillingness to ask for it; ready without reservation or fuss to meet the needs and secure the concerns of their friends: and in fact these people are almost constantly busy more on behalf of others than themselves, mostly with small, but all the same tiresome, boring, difficult chores and services, the sheer number of which, if nothing else, makes up for the smallness of each one, but sometimes in big and very impressive tasks, requiring a corresponding level of attention, effort, and even sacrifice. And it's not that they attach any great importance to their generosity, or insist on it with those they've helped or anyone else, they neither make much of it nor consider it especially worthy of merit (as if they'd been blinded and driven mad by Zeus, as Homer says of Glaucus when he swaps his gold weapons with Diomedes' copper ones): then they expect little or no gratitude, as if they had been obliged to be generous, or as if their generosity cost them nothing; and they never imagine they have the right to claim back what they've given, or that one ought to claim it back; they are extremely reserved about their giving and ask nothing in exchange, and if someone does return them part of what they've given, either spontaneously or at their request, they feel obliged themselves to this person who has only very poorly re-paid the things they did for him.

I've seen all or part of this, sometimes more, sometimes less, in young people with the qualities described above, and not just in those who because of their inexperience of the world and natural kindness, their full hearts and attitude of trust, are simply carried away, transported toward virtue, generosity, magnanimity, finding their greatest pleasure and desire in doing good and being heroic, denying, renouncing, and sacrificing themselves; but even in those disillusioned with the world, who find themselves in the circumstances described above or in some of them, or others like them. All this, then, like I said, I've seen in these young people while they enjoy and feel the benefits of youth, health, and strength and are entirely self-sufficient. But with age, or even before they grow old, if they run into the kind of troubles, accidents, situations, the sort of physical or moral disasters, arising from nature or just bad luck, that undermine their self-sufficiency, placing them regularly or often in need of the support or generosity of others, that weaken or destroy their physical strength and with it their mental energy; then these people, as I have seen myself from experience, previously so compassionate and generous, little by little, in proportion to whatever change of circumstances they have undergone, become insensitive to other people's ills or needs, or comforts, concerned only for themselves, no longer open to feeling compassion, they forget their generosity, and in both attitude and action they entirely reverse their position with regard to these qualities. And not just gradually either, but quickly even, almost instantly, while still in the flower of youth; I myself have seen such changes occur in people overcome by sudden or unexpected disaster, something physical or mental or some reversal of fortune, crushing their spirit and prostrating them in an instant, or in a very short while, leaving them wrecked or very shaky, with their lives now subject to all sorts of troubles and the sad necessity of seeking help from others, their health undermined, body weakened, and other similar changes in their earlier situation. In short, when this kind of instant or abrupt change of circumstances occurs, I have seen an equally instant or abrupt alteration of character and behavior in these people, when it comes to showing compassion, being charitable, or doing good of whatever kind on behalf of others.

And those who by nature, or for whatever reason, from child-hood or adolescence, and from their first entry into the world have always been as the people described above eventually became — I mean weak in both body and mind, fearful, indecisive, disheartened by poverty or for some other reason, whether physical or moral, extrinsic or intrinsic, natural to them or accidental and casual — always or often in need of other people's help, used from an early age to suffering and to seeing their efforts fail and their wishes disappointed, hence always diffident of the world, life and success, and so entirely lacking in self-confidence; more familiar with fear and foreboding than with hope; such people, and anyone like them, partly or entirely, from very early in their lives or from the moment they enter into society, will be more or less alien to compassion and charity, both the actual doing of it and the attitude toward it, showing no inclination or disposition for these virtues, interested as they are entirely in themselves and hardly or not at all able to interest themselves on behalf of others who are in need or in trouble, whether worthy or unworthy of help; and even less able to do anything for anyone not in trouble; thus hardly or not at all able to engage in a real, effective, active friendship, but clever simulators of the same so as to get the help and sympathy they need, and shrewd at turning friendships to their own advantage; in fact, they simulate and dissimulate on a regular basis and in every department. And these qualities become character traits, with the result that in people like this self-regard is never anything other than egoism, and egoism is their main character trait; but this is not their fault, it's a necessity of nature; not that nature directly gave them any more of this miserable quality than it gives other people, but because the circumstances they found themselves in, whether naturally or by accident, led right from the start, naturally and necessarily, to this egoism, perhaps more necessarily and inevitably and to a greater extent than anything prompted by any other cause. See p. 3846.§

   *Weakness in a person will be pleasant and attractive mainly to those who are strong, whether of the same species or not (perhaps because of the mutual attraction of opposites that people say nature has instilled in us). Hence weakness in a woman is more attractive to a man than to other women, and in a child more attractive to adults than to other children. And women are more attractive to men than to other women partly because of their being weaker, etc. And the stronger someone is—there may be other reasons, but this is an important one—the more another's weakness will attract him, always assuming that person is attractive in other ways, etc. This is partly why soldiers, and military nations in general are drawn to women or to τὰ παιδικά [boys], etc. (see Aristotle, *Politics*, 2, Florence 1576, p. 142.). And what we've said of weakness could equally well be said of timidity. When someone, some animal, has other attractions and when the timidity isn't incongruous, it is attractive. For example, in hares, rabbits, and so on. It's especially attractive to those who are strong, either in absolute terms or in relation to this particular creature.

The more courageous a person is, the more timidity is attractive to him, and again this takes us back to what I said about soldiers. Seeing that a person or animal is afraid, and is right to be afraid, and that he / it can't defend him / itself, is an attractive thing and encourages people or animals that are strong and courageous, whether or not of the same species, to spare these elements; except where there are reasons for quite different behavior, as between the wolf and the sheep, etc., reasons that have nothing to do with timidity and courage. And this is at least partly why strong and courageous nations and individuals naturally tend to be more benign than others; while on the contrary it has often been observed that weaker and more fearful peoples and individuals tend to be crueler toward those weaker than themselves, and toward those individuals among themselves who are weaker, etc. And it is an ongoing and widespread observation that fearfulness, cowardice, and weakness are more than happy to keep company with cruelty, harshness, ruthlessness, and toughness, both of attitude and action, etc. (That fear is naturally cruel, because supremely self-centered, and likewise cowardice, is something I've frequently pointed out.) This isn't something you see only in people, but in animals too. And it's highly feasible, if not necessarily correct, when people claim that the lion is generous toward weaker and more fearful animals, etc., except, of course, when nature, I mean a natural hostility, or hunger, etc., spurs it to attack, etc., or sometimes spurs it to attack, albeit not in the case in question, or when nature has destined the weaker animal to be the diet of the stronger, in which case it is highly unlikely that the stronger creature will hold back, or if he does hold back it will only be because he has already eaten enough. These observations can be cross-referenced to others I've made regarding the naturally compassionate disposition of strong people and the naturally harsh, hard-hearted disposition of the weak, etc., and vice versa those other observations can be cross-referenced to these. It is said, and history offers various examples, that when women have achieved power in some way or another, they were and generally are shrewder and grimmer, and to the same degree crueler and less compassionate toward their enemies, or toward others in general, etc., than were or are, would have been or would be, men in similar circumstances. And it is well known that the weakest and more cowardly princes have always been the cruelest when seen in the context of the behavior and temperaments of the times they lived or live in, and of the circumstances in which respectively they found or find themselves, and in line with the various phases and events of each of their lives, etc.

†In fact the more these people are forthright, courageous, not intimidated by another's presence or conversation, frank, open, ready to say what they think and do as they wish, averse to pretense and lying (sometimes excessively so); the more they are vengeful when abused, proudly standing up to anyone who offends, insults, despises, or damages them, the less they are pliant and accommodating with enemies, those who envy them, detractors, slanderers, abusers, and offensive people of any kind; the more even they tend to be rather bullying, verbally or physically, toward people who are neither compassionate nor needy, friends, neutrals, and enemies alike; inclined or quick to anger, that may last quite a while; so the more will they be compassionate and generous toward friends or neutrals (given the occasion and wherewithal, etc., on their part, and the need, or expediency, etc., on the other part) or even toward their enemies and abusers, assuming these people have been defeated, or already punished, or are apologizing and asking forgiveness, or have made good their offense, or even when they have simply been overwhelmed by some serious disaster, and fallen into great need and distress, etc. (Julius Caesar behaved like this, Suetonius recounts). And the opposite is the

case with men of opposite qualities; opposite, I mean, in matters of showing compassion or doing good for whatever person, and in forgiving and forgetting an offense. And by people with opposite qualities I mean men who are fearful, awkward, physically and mentally weak, etc.

‡In fact many of these people enjoy having enemies rather than friends, are happier to be hated than loved, and readily argue with any and everyone, not because they are oversensitive, or misanthropic, or out of a natural hatred for others, etc., but because being at war is their natural state, and they enjoy fighting more than being settled or peaceful, a turbulent life more than a quiet one. And this in the most simple way, without malice, or any dark and hateful passions or character traits. On the contrary, they are very open, sincere, compassionate people, more generous in their giving than others, but even when they are sympathetic and kind to someone, they would much rather have that person as an enemy who fought and hated them. And the same goes for other people they know; they would much rather they were hostile than affectionate or neutral, hence they are always stirring things up and provoking and offending in everything they say and do, so as to have the pleasure of fighting people and being at war, but this entirely without any passion, or with only the mildest of passions, and over the most insignificant trivialities. And since in the normal way of things everyone supposes that things are as they wish them to be, so these people generally cheer themselves up by assuming that others are out to get them, and in imagining that everything other people say or do, however minor, has some evil hostile intention behind it, and grabbing any chance they can to pick a quarrel with anyone, even members of their own family, people they're close to, colleagues, friends. And I'll repeat, they do all this with the utmost simplicity, nobility even, certainly without any deceit or cowardice; without being grim or gloomy (on

the contrary, these people are usually extremely cheerful or tend to cheerfulness), without bile, nor what is called δυσκολία [difficulty] and *morositas* [ill temper], without bitterness, etc., without being too stubborn, behaving too doggedly; on the contrary, these are all characteristics of weak men and losers (and hence rightly attributed in particular to old men and especially to women), without being insatiable, or petulant or frustrated, without being irascible, bullying, and quick-tempered. The strength that comes with youth and health and their general prosperity gives these people such enormous self-confidence that they don't even try to please others or curry favor with them, they're happier opposing them, and they like to think of others as enemies rather than as friends or neutrals, and even to have them as real enemies, more or less, depending on the kind of stakes involved and the physical strength of their opponents. Talking to such people, living with them, being in their company, especially for long periods of time, is extremely difficult and irritating, even though they will never betray you and are always helpful and giving and compassionate and generous. Despite all this they don't have a great capacity to love and are just not made to be friends, while on the other hand they are more capable of making enemies and eager to make them than really able to *be* an enemy, because they are better at anger than hatred, at fighting than hating, at taking revenge rather than going grimly on with something. In fact, such people are almost incapable of hating, and their anger even when it really grips them is pretty bland and brief, perhaps because they are so often angry.

§The essence and strength of this thought is that compassion, charity, sensitivity, etc., which everybody (Rousseau in particular) thinks of as generally a characteristic of the young (young men especially), while insensitivity, harshness, etc., are thought of as characteristics of adults, and even more so of the old (women especially), do not derive from the younger person's innocence, inexperience, and incomplete knowledge of the world, nor the opposite qualities from the experience, worldly knowledge, moral disillusionment, etc., of older people, as most writers suppose and tell us, but from those other physical and moral causes I have discussed here; these are certainly major factors, and quite likely decisive; and if this is not in fact the case for any one of these factors taken singly and measured against the factors of innocence and inexperience, which are indeed extremely important and responsible for the moral differences between the ancients and the moderns, etc., then it certainly is the case when all these causes I'm talking about are taken together. In fact, if we take a man and a woman, equally young and inexperienced, and with all other qualities and circumstances being equal, the man, simply because stronger, etc., is naturally more compassionate, charitable, etc., than the woman and more inclined to compassion and to take an interest in others, etc. Likewise, if we have two young men, equals in every other matter and circumstance, the stronger of the two will be more ready to help others, show compassion, do good, etc., etc.

Philosophical Thoughts—Courage— Pain—Memories of My Life

There are many things, some hardly important, that will prompt a man to put himself in danger, even mortal danger, often deliberately sacrificing himself, his money, his possessions, his comforts, his hopes, etc. But you'll find very few people who even when there are very serious reasons—intense passions even, burning love, etc.—will subject themselves, or are really able to subject themselves, to even quite a small amount of physical pain. People often and easily face mortal danger, willingly and with open eyes, and those same people are unable willingly and knowingly to face certain physical pain.

Man's Inclinations — Comets — Religion.
Cult — Hope and Fear

That fear, as I've said elsewhere, is more natural to man than hope and man more inclined to the one than the other, is evident from the fact that when people don't know the causes of some effect, whether natural or otherwise, they are usually afraid; so that for ignorant people most of all, but also for primitive people, people in the natural state, and children, any effect resulting from a hidden cause is something to be afraid of. Now, when was hope ever so rash? What's more, if ignorance, superstition, etc., led in ancient times or leads today to people seeing some new or unknown effect as an omen for the future, or a sign of something present but as yet unknown, generally those omens and tokens are thought to presage disaster. Let's leave aside eclipses, which may naturally seem frightening to anyone who doesn't know the reason for them, or has never seen one before, etc., and it's quite likely that it was this primitive fear that gave eclipses their reputation of being evil omens, and that made them frightening to people all over the world for so long, right up to the present time, this even after people had understood and understand that the darkening of the sun doesn't last forever but is fleeting, etc. But what is there about a comet that makes it any more frightening than any other heavenly body, or than the Milky Way, etc.? And if people have to see something as a sign or omen, why not of something positive? But you'll find no part of the world where comets were or are reckoned to look forward to anything but disaster. What the ancients called monsters, things that were out of the ordinary, were always reckoned to be bad omens even when there was nothing terrible about them materially or in themselves. Likewise, when a sacrificial victim was found to have no heart, if it's true, as the ancients narrate, that this really happened sometimes, or if it didn't just mistakenly seem to be the case to whoever was inspecting the entrails, etc. All proofs that man is more prone to fear than to hope, more likely to go one way than the other; and that hope is rarely so hasty and irrational as fear; or for sure is so far more rarely, etc. This especially in nature, children, ignorant folk, and natural man.

Courage—Timid People—Timidity—People of Great Talent—Memories of My Life— Theory of the Arts. Practical Part

Many people are both timid and at the same time extremely courageous. I mean, many people lose their nerve when in society, people who wouldn't run away if in danger and who go willingly toward troubles, suffering, hardships, etc.; but they can't deal with the friendly or neutral looks and comments of people they would very easily face as threatening enemies in a battle or a duel. Timidity is directed toward hazards in the mental sphere, courage toward the physical. Timidity fears inner damage and pain, courage confronts outer damage and hardships. The one revolves around things to do with the spirit, the other around things material. And not only does timidity not exclude courage, it actually fosters it; it is from a person's timidity that we can reasonably suppose that he is courageous. Because what timidity generally fears is shame, and shame is what someone who is afraid of danger and who runs away from it is very likely and very often going to have to face. Hence fearing shame, which is so to speak an inner, mental suffering, since it doesn't harm the body or anything in the outer world, but works exclusively on the mind without troubling the physical senses, stops a man from fearing and running away from outer, physical pain so that, when necessary, he will face danger and even certain suffering, preferring outer, material dangers and sufferings to those of the mind and spirit, and putting the spirit, as it were, before the body; choosing to suffer physical pain and loss of possessions, etc., rather than mental pain, opting to die rather than suffer the pangs of shame. In fact it is precisely in this choice that the courage arising from sentiments of honor consists, and together with it all the resulting effects. This courage finds its origin and solid base in timidity, or rather it is itself a kind of timidity, in any event a quality that runs contrary to recklessness, effrontery, and impudence.*

*Timid people (people, that is, who are afraid of shame and prone to δυσωπία, *mauvaise honte* [bashfulness]) are capable not only of facing danger, damage, and sacrifice fearlessly, without running away, but even of going looking for it, of desiring it, loving it, of yearning for death and reaching out for it with both hands. The same moral or physical qualities that often lead to timidity (that is, among others, reflection, delicacy, and profundity of spirit, etc., the which made Rousseau intensely and hopelessly timid), also lead to boredom with life, disillusionment, unhappiness, and ultimately desperation. It's really amazing and pathetic, but nevertheless true, that a man who neither fears nor flees death but yearns for it more than anything else, a man who has despaired of himself and already counts life and human affairs as nothing, a man resolved to die even, nevertheless still fears other people's opinions, still loses his nerve in society, is anxious when there's a risk of making himself ridiculous (in fact, his constant awareness of such risks is precisely what makes him so nervous), and doesn't have the courage to try and do anything to improve his situation or make it less distressing, this out of a fear of making life worse, when actually he no longer cares about life anyway but despairs of it and feels it simply couldn't get any worse, hating it so much already that he wishes more than anything else to be shut of it, or resolutely to throw it away. It's amazing that a man who wishes he was dead and is determined to die, a man who places his hopes in ceasing to exist, who thinks nothing would be better for himself than giving up everything, still reckons he has something to lose and something so important that he fears losing it more than anything else; and that this idea, this fear, makes it impossible for him to do as he feels, and to throw himself desperately into the life that he reckons worthless; and that he much prefers to give up everything, resolutely, and to lose everything, rather than run the risk, as he sees it, of losing the one thing, I mean his reputation, other people's respect, that the timid man, when engaging with society, is constantly afraid of losing, and that he nevertheless knows he will never have, or will lose, through seeming timid; yet the whole situation, the constant fear of losing and the constant and wearisome effort of preserving something he knows he doesn't have, makes him incapable of behaving frankly, even though he's aware that he's bound to lose respect or never have it in the first place unless he sets aside this constant, excessive fear, this constant and excessive caution. All these strange sad contradictions and complications occur (more or less proportionately, etc.) in timid people and the more so the more fastidious-minded they are, this fastidiousness being very often the only or the main reason for their timidity. But as regards still fearing shame while wishing to be dead or being ready to seek death out, this is explained by the fact that this courage, which doesn't spring from physical causes, nor from the ability or habit, natural or acquired, of unthinking spontaneity, but on the contrary from reflection together with a sense of honor, and from a delicacy and fastidiousness of spirit (not, like the other kind of courage, from grossness of spirit) really does prefer death to shame, indeed the more fearful it is of shame as opposed to death, the more deliberately and lucidly it chooses the one rather than the other, preferring not to live than to live tormented by shame.

Christianity—Desire—Happiness That Man Desires— Future Happiness—Pleasure (Theory of)—Hope— Spirit—Memories of My Life

Unfortunately, the hopes Christianity holds out for us are hardly such as to console the man who is unhappy or troubled in this world, or to calm the spirit who finds himself rejected in this life, his desires thwarted, himself scorned and persecuted by men, denied access to pleasures, comforts, conveniences, and temporal honors, crushed by bad luck. The promise and expectation of a very great happiness, supreme and complete, but that, 1., man cannot understand, or imagine, or conceive of, or have any idea, even by approximation, of what kind it might be, 2., he well knows he will never be able to conceive of, or imagine, or have any idea about in this life, and, 3., he knows very well is of a completely different nature from and alien to the happiness he desires in this world, the happiness denied to him here on earth, his yearning for and exclusion from which is the cause of his unhappiness—such a promise, as I was saying, and such an expectation, is really not of a kind to console an unhappy and unfortunate man in this life, to appease and defer his desires and compensate his privations here on earth. The happiness man naturally desires is a temporal happiness, a material happiness, something to be experienced through the senses and by our minds as they are now and as we experience them; in short, a happiness of this life and this existence, not of another life and another existence that we know must be entirely different from this one, and that we cannot conceive of and don't know what qualities it's made up of. Happiness is the perfection and point of arrival of existence. We desire to be happy because we exist. That's how everyone lives. It's obvious, then, that we want to be happy, not any old how, but happy in line with the way we actually exist. Man does not desire happiness absolutely, but human happiness (just like other animals), nor happiness of any kind, but one kind, albeit indefinable. We want it to be supreme and infinite, but of its kind, not infinite in the sense that it includes the happiness of the ox and the vegetable and the Angel and all other kinds of happiness without exception. Only the happiness of God is truly infinite. When it comes to infinity, man desires that his happiness share that attribute with divine happiness, but when it comes to the other qualities and kinds of happiness, man simply wouldn't be able really to desire the happiness God knows. The man who envies another person's clothes or food or house never really envies or desires the immense and complete happiness of God, except insofar as it is immense, and even more insofar as it is complete and perfect. It's obvious that our existence desires its own perfection and its own point of arrival, not those of some other existence we can't conceive of. Our existence, then, desires its own happiness; since if it desired the happiness of another existence, even if ours were then transformed into that, it would be desiring not its own happiness but, as one might say, another's, and hence would have as its true and final point of arrival not itself, but another, which is of its nature impossible for any Being in any action, inclination, or thought, etc. So the happiness man desires is necessarily a happiness that suits him and is proper to his present mode of existence, and one his present existence is capable of. Nor can he ever for any reason stop desiring this happiness, nor for any reason can he ever desire any other happiness than this. It is no more possible for a mortal man truly to desire the happiness of the Blessed than for a horse to desire the happiness of a man, or a plant the happiness of an animal; or again for a herbivorous animal to envy a carnivore its nature or the meat he sees it eating, or envy in man the pleasures of study and knowledge, pleasures the animal can't conceive of, can't understand how they can be pleasures, of what kind they might be, and so on. It's true enough of course that neither man nor animals nor any other creature can exactly define, whether for themselves or for others, the nature, in absolute or general terms, of the happiness they desire; perhaps because no one has ever experienced that happiness, or ever will, and then because endless other concepts of ours, entirely ordinary and humdrum as they may be, remain indefinable for us; especially those that have more to do with physical senses than with ideas; that spring from inclination and appetite, rather than from the intellect, reason, and knowledge; that are more material than mental. Ideas are for the most part definable, but feelings hardly ever are; ideas can be clearly, successfully, and distinctly understood and embraced by the thinking mind, but feelings hardly ever, or never can. All the same, both animals and men well know and understand, or at least feel, that the happiness they want is an earthly thing. Even the infinite to which our spirit tends (in what way and why I have described elsewhere), even that is an earthly infinite, although it can't really happen down here except confusedly in the imagination and the mind, or in the simple desire and appetite of living creatures. Aside from that, there is no one alive who doesn't have some clear, well-defined, and determined desires, whether negative or positive, to the fulfillment of which he always entrusts, consciously or confusedly, but always mistakenly, his happiness and well-being.

Habit—Courage—Human Qualities—Reason— Reflection. Lack of Reflection—Fear

The superiority of nature over reason, of habit (which is second nature) over reflection. My panic in response to every kind of loud bang, not only dangerous ones (e.g., thunder), but entirely innocuous ones too (e.g., firecrackers at parties), a fear that strangely and irresistibly took hold of me not in infancy but in adolescence, when I was already well able to reason and reflect, and in fact did so, but without ever managing to shake off this fear, despite the fact that all logic showed me that it was entirely unreasonable. I didn't believe I was in danger, I knew there was no danger and nothing to fear, but I feared this nothing just as if I had known, believed, and reflected the opposite.* Neither reason nor reflection could free me from this completely unreasonable fear, because it was caused by nature. Nor certainly was I particularly stupid or unthinking, or one of those people who live without using their heads, or who do not particularly feel the force of reason and are less used to reasoning and blindly follow their instincts and natural tendencies. But what reason and reflection in opposition to nature were completely incapable of doing, nature itself and habit eventually did for me. Because with time, actually in quite a brief space of time, finding myself forced on certain occasions to hear these loud bangs often and close by, I lost this innate and extremely stubborn fear to the extent that not only did I start to take pleasure in something that had previously been unreasonably hateful and frightening to me, but I stopped feeling afraid and began to love even the kinds of explosions that I should reasonably have been afraid of; neither reason nor reflection, which had previously failed to free me from this natural fear, was later able, nor are they now, to make me fear or even just not love something that from nature or habit, and unreasonably, I now love and do not fear. Nor am I, as I have said, the kind of person who doesn't reflect on things, nor have I stopped thinking even now about these things when the occasion occurs, but reflection never succeeds in having me conceive a fear that is no longer natural to me. And what I say here of myself, I'm sure has happened and happens to thousands of other people every day, either with regard to just one of the two parts of my story, or to both. What reflection, however insistent, simply cannot achieve, lack of reflection can and does.†

*Now someone facing danger who needs to have his courage bolstered, or to be fed examples of another's courage in the same situation, and who otherwise would be afraid, is hardly courageous, or not on this occasion. And someone who, in order not to be afraid, needs to believe that there is no danger, no reason to fear, that is, and to talk down the prospect of danger and to believe that this danger, this reason for being afraid is slight, or less, or smaller than it is, and otherwise would be afraid, is hardly courageous, because no one fears something he doesn't believe he has any reason to fear, and no one is afraid if he feels, rightly or wrongly, that there is no prospect of danger, however minimal the prospect may be, or unreasonable, a product of instinct almost or passion.

†And very often the unreflecting nature of children and ignorant or inexpert folk, etc., achieves as much, and just as well, or even better, as do reflection, prudence, forward-planning, awareness, ability, readiness, etc., and the presence of spirit acquired in practical experience, etc., gets the same results as a more reflective man might after very long consideration, and where speed is of the essence, it will identify and achieve its goals as rapidly if not more rapidly than can a habit of reflection, etc.

Courage—Memories of My Life

Laughing when danger presents itself, becoming exaggeratedly cheerful, or more than one was a moment before, or moving from gloominess to jollity, getting talkative when one is generally quiet, or breaking a silence you had for some reason been keeping; joking, hopping around, singing, and suchlike are hardly, as people suppose, signs of courage, but on the contrary are signs of fear. They indicate that a person needs to distract himself from the idea of danger, or, to be precise, to dispel the idea by convincing himself that there is no danger, or that the danger isn't serious. This is what the person who shows signs of unusual cheerfulness in such situations is trying to do: fool himself by showing himself he has nothing to fear, since his behavior runs contrary to the normal, proper, unmediated reaction to fear. In order not to fear, man tries to convince himself that he isn't afraid, so that then he can deduce that there is no sufficient or necessary reason for fear. It's quite normal for this passion to prompt people to do things that run contrary to the reactions it would usually provoke if unmediated, but both responses are equally caused by real fear. However, one kind of response is mainly, or seen from a certain angle, fake; the other genuine. Fear prompts people to act out what is almost a pantomime for themselves. That's why when you're alone in the dark in places, paths, situations that are or seem dangerous, it's common for people to sing, not so much to make out and pretend one is in company, or to keep oneself company (as they say), but because singing seems to be absolutely typical of someone who isn't afraid: so precisely someone who is afraid sings. (On this subject, see a very pertinent passage in Magalotti that I mentioned in the opening pages of these thoughts, around the beginning of 1819 if I'm not mistaken.) The same logic (more than the need for distraction) lies behind the fact that when there is, or people think there is, a common danger, whether real or entirely imaginary, they like to hear other people sing, and are cheered and comforted on seeing others going about their usual business, realizing or believing that these people don't think there's any danger, or anything that would cause them to neglect or change their routine, or whatever they were doing up to now, or whatever they would have done if there hadn't been this danger; or just seeing that they are not afraid, undaunted rather, etc. Seeing, or supposing, courage in others, or their acting as if not in danger, transmits courage to someone who is afraid. In the same way, showing oneself that one is not afraid is a way of building up one's courage, either by convincing oneself that one is not in danger, or making a show to oneself of being courageous and not fearing whatever danger there may actually be.

**Harmony of Nature—Compassion—Weakness—
Delicacy of Forms—Women—Children—Grace—
Pleasure, Theory of—Nature—Memories of
My Life—Theory of the Arts. Speculative Part**

I've remarked elsewhere that weakness is itself pleasant when it doesn't clash with the nature of the subject who is weak, or rather with the way we are used to seeing and thinking of the species this subject belongs to; or when it does clash, if all the same it doesn't actually destroy the essential aspect of this nature, and doesn't clash too much: in short, when the weakness suits either the subject or the idea we've formed of this subject in its perfected state, and fits in with the subject's other qualities, in line with this same idea we have (as is the case with children and women); or in cases when it doesn't suit and doesn't fit, if it nevertheless doesn't destroy the apparent propriety of our idea of the subject, but remains within the terms of that kind of friction we can call charming (this according to my theory of charm), as when weakness occurs in men, or occurs more markedly than is normal in women, etc. As a rule, weakness is attractive and likable and beautiful within an overall beauty. Never-theless, it can also be (and sometimes actually is) likable, beauti-ful, and attractive in an overall ugliness, not because it is located in ugliness, but simply because it is what it is, this so long as the weakness is not itself in part or in whole the cause of the ugliness. Now the fact that weakness is of itself, assuming nothing outside the weakness prevents this, naturally attractive, is a charming act of providence on nature's part, for since nature has made self-regard the dominant inclination in every creature and since, as I've shown elsewhere, one typical and inevitable consequence of self-regard in every creature is the general tendency to hate others, you would have thought that weak creatures would all too often fall victims to strong creatures. But since weakness is naturally and in itself a source of pleasure and attraction to others, it induces those others to love the subject who displays it, and they love it in response to their own self-regard, because they derive pleasure from it.

Compassion — Narrative

Since, as I've shown elsewhere, the epic poet (and likewise the dramatist, the novelist, etc., but also the historian) absolutely has to get readers to like a character he wants them to be interested in, and this any way he can, no matter what, and then enormously to like the character he wants them to be most interested in, it's worth pointing out that one of the best ways of achieving this effect is by subjecting his character to hardship, something that will multiply any likability he already has by many times and is often capable of making an unlikable character likable, even if he deserves the trouble he runs into and much more so when he doesn't. The most likable man who undeservedly undergoes the most extreme hardship becomes the most likable subject one can imagine. The likable man who deservedly undergoes hardship is always more interesting, and more easily the object of affection and sympathy, than a character who is not likable and undeservedly undergoes hardship, a figure who quite likely won't arouse the reader's sympathy or interest at all (as very often happens), even when his hardships are extreme, while the likable character's are minimal, in which case the latter is bound to arouse our sympathy and prove more likable than he ordinarily would. But let's not waste time with all these subtleties and distinctions. When it comes to the main Hero of the adventure who constitutes the real subject of the poem, his unhappiness must be accidental and must, as I've explained and shown elsewhere, be resolved at the end, leaving him in a state of happiness. These observations, then, powerfully confirm my argument that in the epic poem the poet must provide two areas of interest in the work if he wants his poem to be supremely engaging and to produce the maximum effect; they also justify and increase our admiration for Homer's strategy in *The Iliad*. Because since you can't have maximum engagement in the poem without maximum likability and since hardship is absolutely the main source of likability, its peak and perfection almost, and since the hero of the adventure cannot be subject to an overwhelming, total, and final unhappiness, the only thing to do if we want the poem to be supremely engaging is to use the form to create two focuses of interest, separating out the one interest from the other by introducing a second hero who is supremely likable and undergoes supreme hardship;

his total misery will produce this second interest we've mentioned, which will revolve around that misery, always tending toward it and moved along by it throughout the whole poem, thus making the work supremely engaging and such as to sustain that engagement in the reader's mind long after he has put the book down, etc. This is what Homer did in *The Iliad*, where Hector's qualities and actions, and his supreme, complete, final catastrophe, make him supremely likable and hence supremely engaging. As for the other protagonist, Achilles, the Hero of the adventure (let's call him that for brevity's sake), Homer couldn't doom him to such unhappiness and calamity, especially considering the nature and opinions of the times that placed success beyond all other virtues and that even (as I've remarked elsewhere) pronounced a man good or evil, deserving or undeserving, depending on his good or bad luck, since they couldn't accept that either bad luck or good could befall people who didn't deserve it. But so far as was possible, Homer did what he could to stimulate the most positive feelings in Achilles' regard, above all compassion, the most tender of emotions, and mother or catalyst of love. This not only with the accidental calamity of his friend Patroclus's death, and other similar hardships, but also by foreseeing, as though in the distant future, the final tragedy and unhappy destiny of the brave Achilles, who by an irreversible decree of fate was doomed to die in the flower of his youth, this as the price of his glory, something he had knowingly and freely chosen, preferring glory and an early death to a long life without honor. It is a sublime trait and one that completes the poetic and epic quality of Achilles' character, virtue, courage, greatness of soul, etc., and that makes him at the last a supremely likable and engaging figure.

Compassion

Tasso doesn't even stop at making Rinaldo wholly guilty of a serious albeit forgivable crime resulting from a passion typical and worthy of a man, almost obligatory in a young man, and even more so in one with a noble spirit, ready of hand and heart; I mean anger in reaction to insult. It's a passion that, especially in these circumstances, makes a man extremely likable, despite the grim consequences it can lead to, and despite the fact that it also comes in for blame (since it's one thing to blame something and another to hate it), and that philosophers and educators say it should be checked or entirely rooted out of the mind. For sure in a young man, this passion is almost always much more likable and engaging than patience. You can see this in life every day. However, Rinaldo's character is much more like Achilles', and much more poetic, likable and engaging than Aeneas's. Or if nothing else one might rightly say that Rinaldo is more likable than Aeneas to the same degree that Aeneas is more likable than Goffredo. Aeneas has gone through and continues to go through many calamities before reaching happiness. Yet he hardly arouses a great deal of compassion, because the poet set out to make him more admirable than likable; and again because one can't feel much compassion for a person who hardly seems to suffer in the midst of his troubles and calamities.

The Ancients — Civilization — Process of Civilization — Opinions (Diversity of) — Pleasure (Theory of) — Pleasures — Vagueness

It's well known that imagination, opinion, prejudice, etc.,

always have a huge influence on love, even physical love, and on the emotions that a man feels in particular toward a woman, or a woman toward a man. One thing that has a specially powerful influence on love, not just platonic or sentimental love, but even physical love directed at specific individuals, is a sense of mystery; everything that serves to make the object of the lover's attention vague and unknown and hence to give rein to his imagination to build up an idea, as it were, around this object. So everything to do with the anyway likable virtues and qualities of the beloved's personality will contribute enormously to love and desire, even physical desire, and this is especially true where that personality is deep, melancholy, and sentimental, or where it seems to contain within more than it shows without. Because the mind and its qualities, especially those I've just mentioned, are hidden things, that other people can't know, and hence they give rise to imaginings, and to vague and indeterminate ideas. Fusing with the natural desire that an individual of one sex will have for an individual of the other, these ideas and imaginings give infinite urgency to this desire, enormously increasing the pleasure experienced on satisfying it. The mysterious and naturally indeterminate ideas—having to do with the beloved's mind and arising from the parts and qualities that belong to his or her spirit, especially if those qualities have something deep and hidden and unclear about them, and promise or hint at other hidden and lovable parts and qualities etc.—these ideas, I was saying, fusing with the manifest, well-defined ideas connected with the material presence of the beloved, and conferring on them a sense of vagueness and mystery, make them infinitely more beautiful, and the body of the lovable or beloved person infinitely more lovable, precious, desirable, and dear to the lover when the love is consummated.

Generally, one of the main factors that have given rise to a love that is sentimental, spiritual, etc. (aside, that is, from the one noted in the thought to which this thought refers back), is that as men became more and more civilized there was a consequent and proportional increase in the consistency, effectiveness, worth, importance, extension, activity, influence, strength, power, and capacity of the inner and spiritual part of man. So for the first time people came to recognize and suppose that man was possessed of a hidden invisible part that primitive man either did not imagine was there at all, or imagined it only dimly, hardly distinguishing it from the visible and physical part; then they began to give it the same importance as the outer part; then even greater importance, and still more and more importance as time passed, so that today, if nature didn't oppose the idea (and in the end nature can never be totally extinguished or overcome), people would hardly consider anything in man in general or in individuals in particular but the inner life, and when one referred to man, one would mean nothing but the spirit of man. Now, in proportion to this spiritualization of things and of the idea of man, and indeed of man himself, there has also been a growing spiritualization of love, a process which makes love both source and territory of more vague ideas and more indefinite emotions perhaps than any other passion, this despite the fact that in the beginning and, as far as its end purpose is concerned, even today, love was / is perhaps at the same time the most material and clearly defined of the passions, one common, at least as far as its nature is concerned, to animals and to the most animal and stupid of men, those least involved in any mental life. So much so that in recent years, as this process of spiritualization reached its climax, we have seen in our lifetimes the birth—or at least seen it become common for the first time—of that love which, being new, has a new name and is called sentimental love. It's a love that the ancients knew nothing at all about, or that under the name Platonic, manifesting itself occasionally in some rare spirits, or discussed by scholars and philosophers, had until recently been considered a fable, an invention of the mind, a chimera, or a miracle, something that runs contrary to universal nature, or something impossible, or absolutely extraordinary, or a word without any meaning, a confused idea. And indeed until very recently that's just what it was, nothing but an extremely confused idea, something philosophers maybe named but could not conceive of, and as such something the wisest thinkers chuckled over and reckoned incapable of ever really existing in a well-defined form. This excessive spiritualization of love in modern times, which we now call sentimental love, corresponds to the overwhelming spiritualization of human life that has taken place in recent years.

How this spiritualization of all things human came about and had to come about, and how the spiritualization of love developed alongside it, always in exact proportion, until it reached its maximum intensity, and along with that too the vague and the indefinite, which are typical of this passion and of the emotions of one sex toward the other, is evident enough and easy to explain in the terms mentioned above. In the beginning man considered only the outward appearance of himself and other men and naturally of women too, and likewise women when they were looking at men.

But as the process of civilization began and the idea of the spirit was born, because of the strength and activity that the inner part began to acquire and develop, with the inner life and the idea of the spirit gradually equaling in importance the outer life and the idea of the body, then slowly prevailing over it, overwhelming it, so the individual of one sex necessarily began first to take the spirit of the beloved of the other sex into account and then to give it the same importance as he gave the body and finally more importance, at least in a certain sense and a certain way. So to the individual of one sex the lovable object of the other was no longer simply a material object, as previously, but an object made up of spirit and body, a hidden part and a manifest part, and with the passing of time an object more spiritual than material, more hidden and fantasized than manifest and perceived through the senses, more inner than outer. And as those ideas that have to do with the inner, hidden part of man are naturally vague and indefinite, so the idea of the beloved object, considered in the way described, necessarily began to have something mysterious about it, fusing together a consideration of both spirit and body; and as the inner grew in importance with respect to the outer, so the idea of the beloved inevitably became ever more mysterious, until finally it partook more of the mystic, the indefinite, and the vague than the evident and determined. Hence the emotions and ideas that belong to the passion love become more and more indefinite in proportion as man becomes more civilized (and hence no doubt love has become incomparably more pleasurable); so much so that, even though the principle of love remains necessarily the same today as it was for primitive man and as it is among uncivilized people, as it is and always was among animals, that is to say as material and animal as ever, nevertheless by bringing together the spiritual and the material, this passion has become so different in modern man than in primitive man or savages that a love which is truly sentimental doesn't seem to have anything to do with the love of savages or animals, but to be of a quite different and distinct nature, principle, and origin. And today even the least Platonic and most sensual of loves is still largely and necessarily spiritual in its ideas and feelings, and hence largely imagined and thus vague and indefinite; and in one way or another even the most brutish of people always give considerable importance to a hidden part of the object loved, lovable, or enjoyed, a part that accompanies, animates and strictly belongs to, embraces and is one with, that part, those limbs that they desire, and enjoy, or that they consider lovable and desirable; because that part is indeed there, and is an extremely important element in this beloved object's being, so that however brutal or insensitive the beloved may also be, the inner life remains an extremely large part of his or her being; and the lover sees this clearly enough every day. I'm speaking here of lovers and their beloveds who, however brutal, uncultured, and mostly closed to the spirit, are nevertheless part of civilized society.

Courage—Reflection. Lack of Reflection

There are two kinds of courage, each the opposite of the other. The one that arises directly from thinking and is characteristic of it, the other from not thinking. The first, however hard one tries, is always weak, wavering, brief, and not to be trusted, either by others or the person doing the thinking and trying.

Communicating Pleasures to Others

"A great pleasure, if not talked about, is not a whole pleasure."
Machiavelli, *The Golden Ass*, ch. 4, ll. 86–87.

Compassion, Beneficence—Memories of My Life

People who are cheerful, whether by nature or habit, or in response to circumstance and occasion, are usually willing to give to others or to help them and sympathize with them, while gloomy people are the opposite, or certainly less willing. I've written about this at length elsewhere.

Self-Regard—Upbringing. Teaching—Moral Etiquette— Social Machiavellianism—Timid People—Men of Great Talent—Vitality, Sensibility—Memories of My Life

People who speak freely and frankly, especially the ones who look down on everybody, would seem to have more self-regard and self-esteem than others, while timid people appear to have less. The opposite is the case. Out of an excess of self-regard, and thinking far too much of themselves, timid people are always afraid of making a poor impression and losing other people's respect, or alternatively far too eager to make a good impression and win respect, hence they can't see beyond the risks to their honor, sense of themselves, and self-regard; blocked and obsessed as they are by these concerns, they lack courage and never act boldly.

Christianity—Education. Teaching—Sensitive Young
People—Youth—Men's Inclinations—Monks—Pleasure,
Theory of—Self-Sacrifice—Memories of My Life

*Il est aisé de voir la prodigieuse révolution que cette époque
(celle du Christianisme) dut produire dans les moeurs. Les femmes,
presque toutes d'une imagination vive et d'une âme ardente, se livrè-
rent à des vertus qui les flattoient d'autant plus, qu'elles étoient
pénibles. Il est presque égal pour le bonheur de satisfaire de grandes
passions, ou de les vaincre. L'âme est heureuse par ses efforts; et
pourvu qu'elle s'exerce, peu lui importe d'exercer son activité con-
tre elle-même.* [It's easy to see the prodigious revolution that this
era (the Christian era) inevitably brought with it in people's habits.
The women, almost all of lively imagination and fervent spirit, gave
themselves over to virtue, and the more suffering was involved the
better they felt about it. They find just as much happiness overcoming a grand passion as satisfying it. The soul takes pleasure in
its efforts and as long as it is making an effort it hardly matters if that
effort is being made against itself.] Thomas, *Essai sur les femmes*,
Oeuvres, Amsterdam 1774, tome 4.

Compassion, Charity—Interest in Others—Mortification—
Sensitive People—Memories of My Life

Habitual unhappiness, or even just being constantly deprived
of pleasures and circumstances that feed our self-regard, will in the
long run extinguish every more pleasant imagining, every positive
emotion, all life, activity, and strength, and almost every faculty we
may have. The reason for this is that a person in such a position,

after a first phase of pointless despair, and ferocious or painful resistance to the inevitable, will finally be reduced to a calm state,
at which point he has no other expedient for living, nor do nature
and time produce anything else in him than a habit of continually
repressing and mortifying his self-regard, this to make the unhappiness less hurtful, more bearable, and more compatible with a state
of calm. So the less one cares about or is sensitive toward oneself the
better. Now this is a perfect death of the mind and of its faculties. A
man who takes no interest in himself is incapable of taking an interest in anything, because nothing of whatever kind can interest a
man if not in relation, more or less immediate and evident, to himself. The beauties of nature, music, the finest poetry, world events,
happy or sad as they may be, the fortunes and misfortunes of others,
even close friends and family, make no lively impression on him,
don't revive him, don't rouse him, don't evoke any image, feeling or
interest at all, nor give him pleasure or pain, even if just a few years
previously they would have filled him with excitement and stirred
him to intense creativity. He is amazed and stupefied by his own
sterility, lassitude, and coldness. Extremely capable as he once was,
he has now become incapable of anything, of no use to himself or
to others. When self-regard loses its impetus, life is finished. Every
mental strength is extinguished along with hope. I mean along with
this quiet desperation, because a furious desperation is actually full
of hope, or at least desire, and yearns and craves for happiness precisely as it takes up arms or poison against itself. But in a mind used
to seeing its wishes forever thwarted, a mind reduced, whether by
reflection or habit or both, to numbing and repressing those wishes,
desire is as dead as dead can be. The man who desires nothing for

himself and does not love himself is no good to anyone. All the pleasures and pains, the feelings and actions that the things we mentioned above, nature and all the rest, used to inspire in him, were
referred in one way or another to himself, and their intensity con-
sisted in a lively awareness of himself. Likewise, when making sacrifices on behalf of others, he had drawn his energy from this same
return in attention to himself, not from anything else. But bereft of
either ferocity or misanthropy, likewise of rancor and resentment,
and even his egoism, this person who only a short while ago was
so kind is now insensitive to tears and closed to all compassion.
He may come to someone's assistance, but will not sympathize. He
may give to charity or help someone, but only out of a cold sense of
duty or because it is the thing to do, without a feeling that prompts
him to do it and without eliciting any pleasure from it. Real, emotionless neglect of oneself means neglect of everything and hence
incapacity to do anything, and annihilation of the spirit, were it by
nature the greatest and most fertile that ever was.

The effect that produces this unhappiness, is, as I said, the
situation where someone never feels or sees the prospect of any
appearance of happiness, any pleasant future, any pleasure great
or small, any success, whether fleeting or lasting, any caress or trib-
ute from people or things. Permanently bereft of praise, self-regard
inevitably withdraws from both things and people (however kind
and philanthropic it previously was), and the man who is inured
to seeing nothing for himself in life or in the world, will grow used
to not engaging with it and, as everything becomes unimportant to
him, the greatest genius will become sterile and incapable even of

the kind of things that people who by nature are less gifted and prolific, indeed dry and inept, can do with no problem at all. And as
his self-regard is continually denied any illusion or success, so his
habit of neglect, his ineptitude and distaste for life, is confirmed.
It's a sad characteristic of genius that the more lively its self-regard
was in the first place, and hence the more needy and avid of praise
and pleasures and hopes, so all the more easily it falls into this depressed state (which if typical of anyone is typical of the genius); at
this point such a person is less likely to appreciate and make do with
what is quite enough for others, more ready to take offense and suffer for jibes that common people don't feel.*

> **C'est ainsi que les grands Hommes découvrent, comme par
> inspiration, des vérités que les hommes ordinaires n'entendent quel-
> quefois qu'au bout de cent ans de pratique et d'étude; et celui qui
> démontre ces vérités après eux, acquiert encore une gloire immor-
> telle.* [It is thus that great Men discover, as though by inspiration,
> truths that ordinary men arrive at, if at all, only after a hundred
> years of experience and study; and the person who later reveals
> these truths goes on to achieve immortal glory.] Thomas, loc. cit.,
> p. 37. *Sa géometrie étoit si fort au dessus de son siècle qu'il n'y avoit
> réellement que très peu d'hommes en état de l'entendre. C'est ce
> qui arriva depuis à Newton; c'est ce qui arrive à presque tous les
> grands hommes. Il faut que leur siècle coure après eux pour les at-
> teindre.* [His geometry was so far beyond that of his century that
> in reality there were only a very few people who could understand
> it. The same thing happened to Newton; it happens to all great
> men. Their century has to run after them to catch up.] Ibid., note
> 22, p. 143.

Objects of Compassion—Compassion—
Memories of My Life

Compassion arising in response to beauty, even toward people
who for many reasons don't deserve it, then perpetuated by pos-
terity, which people always assume is a good judge. See Thomas loc.
cit., ch. 26, pp. 46–47.

Social Machiavellianism—Tiberius (Character of)—
Handbook of Practical Philosophy—Memories of My Life

Tiberius's contradictory behavior in the empire, his first being
not merely affable, benign, and moderate, but even humble, in short
more than civil (see Suetonius, *Tiberius*, chs. 24–33), having difficulty accepting the gift of empire, etc., then later tyrannical, is attributed to profound political dissembling and pretense. I can't see
anything fake or artificial in what he did. Tiberius, unlike Caesar,
was definitely a timid man by nature. Unlike both Caesar, who from
his youth on was continually working his way up through the ranks,
training his mind and character toward greater and greater respon-
sibilities, and Augustus, who likewise was already in positions of
command from an early age, Tiberius was born into a private family
and spent his youth and adulthood under threat from Augustus and
his family, who were suspicious of his intentions; as a result and in
considerable danger, he withdrew to Rhodes to escape the situation or at least limit the danger and stayed there eight years; hence
neither his mind nor character had been prepared for power when
fortune dropped it on his plate. But at the beginning he was modest,
timid and humble rather, even after every fear had been put behind

him, as Suetonius* says very clearly (ch. 26, paragraph 6), nor was there any dissembling here: all I see is a man used to succumbing, used to being afraid and to avoiding giving offense, who now, finding himself in power, still preserves these habits of fear and avoidance. He loses the habit over time and with the ongoing experience of his power and of other people's submissive, even cringing, attitude to him. There's no question of his pulling off a mask; this is a change of character and nature due to a change of circumstances. Tiberius was certainly cruel, because cowardly and weak.† This was why power transformed him into a tyrant, because his nature was such that the experience of leadership inevitably made him a cruel sort of leader. But there was no pretense involved.

*Suetonius, meantime, like others, attributes Tiberius's moderation at the beginning of his government to calculation and deception.

†Teodorus Gadarenus, Tiberius's rhetoric teacher when he was a boy, *subinde in obiurgando* appellabat *eum* "πηλὸν αἵματι πεφ-υραμένον" [soon afterward denounced him as "mud mixed with blood," Suetonius, ch. 57]. And Suetonius himself says his character was *saeva ac lenta natura* [of a cruel and sluggish nature] (ibid., beginning).

Courage—Childhood—Parents. Father's House—Youth— Man's Inclinations—Religion. Cult—Memories of My Life

A weak, depressed man facing all kinds of dangers, disasters, and fears will naturally suppose, imagine, pretend, often with no good reason, that another person is particularly sensible, wise and prudent, knowing and discerning, possessed of a shrewdness and experience superior to his own; then, watching this person whenever things get tough, he will draw comfort or grow frightened in response to the other's looking happy or sad, depressed or courageous, and calmly rely on his authority, without any other reason; very often, in the gravest of dangers and most depressing of situations, he will even find consolation and take heart merely because of the high hopes and optimism, manifestly false or apparently baseless, that he sees, or supposes he sees, in this person; or again just because the other has a happy or determined look on his face. Children, particularly young children, very often behave this way with their parents. I behaved this way with my father even when I'd reached an age of stability and maturity; so much so that in every difficult situation, every alarm, just so as to work out, if nothing else, how anxious or afraid I should be, I would first wait to see, or speculate on, his state of mind, and want to know how he saw and judged the situation, neither more nor less, as if I myself were incapable of judging it; and if I saw that, whether really or apparently, he wasn't worried, I would cheer up again, excessively, with a completely blind submission to his authority, or faith in his capacity to provide. And if I was away from him, I very often felt a physical, though unreasoned, desire for the shelter he offered. And it's something that's been observed, seen, experienced, a thousand times how soldiers, even the most hardened veterans, when facing dangers, emergencies, disasters in battle, will hang on the opinions, words, actions, and facial expressions of some captain of theirs, even someone young and immature, who has won their confidence; and depending on how they see, or imagine they see, him reacting to the situation will hope or fear, feel anxious or encouraged, take heart or despair. This is why it's so important that a captain show determination and hide his distress or fear in situations where there's every reason to be distressed or fearful. And this human tendency is again one of the reasons why man has so universally and willingly embraced and sustained, and still does so today, the idea of a provident God, a being superior to ourselves in both wisdom and intellect, who looks after us in every circumstance, directs all our doings, and in whose providence we can trust for the success of all our projects. The belief in a being infinitely wiser and more knowing than ourselves, who looks after and continually guides everything that happens, and all to the good, even the things that to us seem most damaging, and who watches over our destinies; and all this for reasons and in ways we know nothing about and that we could never in any way discover or understand, with the result that we don't have to think about it at all; this belief, for absolutely everyone, but particularly for people who are weak and unhappy, is a greater comfort than any other ever could be: and it's a comfort that proceeds from and consists in this and this alone; a reliance on, a yielding to, and a blind confidence in the authority, wisdom, and providence of someone else.

Habit—Compassion, Charity—Moral Intermittency— Memories of My Life

"Moral intermittency." Passions and qualities that are intermittent. "Let me add that this hateful passion" (miserliness), "often coming as it does from a weak constitution, may develop in relation to physical infirmities. A woman who for six months of the year was subject to moods and depression was also grossly mean during that period; but no sooner had her bodily functions recovered their harmony than she had people worshiping her for her great generosity." Alibert, *Physiologie des passions*, in *Nuovo Ricoglitore*, Milan, issue 23, p. 788. This observation can be extended enormously. If we observe ourselves, we'll find that we are all subject to the same intermittency. For myself, being weak and infirm, I'm inclined to be self-centered, but I'm a thousand times more self-centered in winter than in summer; when ill than when in good health, and looking forward to the future; I'm more open to compassion and more likely to take an interest in others and to help them when some success has brought me self-confidence, or pleasure, than when I'm feeling down or depressed. And how much could be said about this same intermittency if we took into consideration not just moral qualities, but intellectual and social skills as well, whether innate or acquired!

Children and Young People — Memories of My Life

Childhood and youth would appear to have an innate, natural tendency to destroy, and maturity and old age to preserve. I'm not deducing this just from seeing how young men tend to squander and ruin the fortunes that more experienced people accumulate, preserve, and increase ("Lack of Consideration and Carelessness about the Future"), something easily explained by the fact that young people tend to be overconfident and don't think or worry about the future, while old people are careful, cautious, and forever worried about the future. But one can see the tendencies I mentioned even in areas where fear and confidence, prudence and imprudence don't come into it. A child and a young man will frequently take pleasure in killing a fly or other small animal, will even make quite an effort to catch it, for no other reason or purpose than because it amuses them; only very rarely will they take pleasure, or will it even come into their heads, to save some animal they see in danger, and could save with no effort at all. An adult or older man rarely takes pleasure in killing and often is happy to save such creatures on seeing them in danger, especially if he can do so without any trouble to himself. And both young and old seem to do these things instinctively, without thinking about them. Then it's obvious that young people are inclined to novelty, and not only eager to make real changes, but even just to kill off the old, or to see it killed off; while more experienced people on the contrary are eager to preserve things as they are. So one might say that nature, ever intent and attentive as much to destroy as to produce and preserve, has given those still growing and coming up in the world the responsibility and urge to destroy things, to make space for themselves almost; and given those who are past their peak and on their way to leaving the world the task of producing and preserving, so that when they go the space they've occupied will be full, they'll leave things behind in their place, things that will stand in for them when they are gone.

Compassion—Weakness—Drama—Epic—Interest in
Poetry—Tasso and Dante—Memories of My Life—
Theory of the Arts. Practical Part

Of our greatest poets, two, Dante and Tasso, were extremely
unlucky. Both have graves that can be visited, both outside their
homelands. But though I wept over Tasso's grave, over Dante's I
didn't feel any sympathy at all; and I imagine it's the same for everyone. This despite the fact that neither I nor others have anything but
the highest opinion of Dante, admiration rather, perhaps a greater
admiration (and rightly so) than for Tasso. What's more, while
there's no doubt that Dante's misfortunes were real and considerable, we can hardly be sure that Tasso's weren't, at least very largely,
imaginary, such is the scarcity and uncertainty of the information
that we have on the subject, so confused and constantly contradictory is Tasso's manner of writing about them. But in Dante we see
a strong-willed man, a man with the personality to deal with adversity and come through it; a man, what's more, who faced and fought
hardship, necessity, and fate. Which makes him all the more admirable no doubt, but all the less likable or likely to arouse our sympathy. In Tasso we see someone overwhelmed by his troubles, a loser,
beaten, someone who collapsed in the face of adversity, constantly
suffering and grieving, excessively so. Even if all his troubles did
turn out to be entirely imaginary and unreal, his unhappiness was
real enough. Indeed, it would hardly be wrong to say that though he
wasn't so unfortunate as Dante, he was definitely unhappier. (This
can be applied to the epic, and to drama, etc.)

Upbringing. Teaching — French — Moral Etiquette —
the English — Italy — the Spanish — National Arrogance —
the Germans — Memories of My Life

We are all naturally inclined to think of ourselves as equal to
those superior to us, superior to those equal to us, and incomparably more important than our inferiors; in short, to think of ourselves as far more deserving than others, and this excessively and
unreasonably so. This is universal nature and comes from a source
common to everyone. But there is another source of pride in oneself and contempt for others that we [Italians] know nothing about;
something that having begun in infancy becomes, through habit,
natural and proper to a person; this is, at least among the French
and English, the regard they have for their own nation. So it is that
the most sympathetic, well-educated, open-minded Frenchman or
Englishman, finding himself in the company of foreigners, simply
cannot help wholeheartedly and sincerely supposing that he is in
the company of someone inferior to himself (this regardless of other
circumstances), cannot help despising more or less all other nations
in general, and cannot help in one way or another making this opinion of his own superiority plain to everybody. This is a stimulus to,
and a very distinct source of, pride and self-esteem, based on prejudice and a low opinion of others, a stimulus no civilized people can
have or form a precise idea about but the abovementioned English
and French. The Germans, who could with equal right enjoy the
same sentiments, are held back by their divisions, their not having
a German nation. The Russians feel they are half barbarians; the
Swedes, Danes, and Dutch that they are too small and can hardly

achieve very much. In the times of Charles V and Philip II the Spanish no doubt felt, as history shows, very much as do the French and English today, and with equal right; perhaps they still feel that, though with no right at all; likewise the Portuguese, but who, when it comes to civilized peoples, thinks that the Spanish or Portuguese count for anything? The Italians perhaps had this confidence (it seems they definitely did) in the fifteenth and sixteenth centuries, as well as for a part of the centuries before and after; this thanks to their culture, which they well knew, and others agreed, was superior to any in Europe. As for Italians today I shan't say anything; I'm not sure if they have it or not.

Feeling that foreigners are inferior, looking down on them, and treating them accordingly is something that from long habit has become as natural and as much part of their identity for the French and English, as talking down to poor and common people and treating them as naturally inferior is to someone born into a rich and noble family: to the point that even the kindest-hearted and most philosophically minded man in the world, if born into this condition, will treat other people this way, unless, that is, he becomes aware of the situation and makes a determined effort to behave differently: because this sense of his superiority to these other people doesn't depend on his reason or his having wanted it that way.

There's no doubt that this high opinion the French and English have of themselves can be extremely useful to them. It would be useful even to someone who had no reason for having it. Having a high opinion of oneself is the first precondition both for morality and for noble and honorable ambitions and actions. On the other hand, since knowing that others think us inferior and have a certain contempt for whatever we do is always irksome, there's no doubt that seeing this high level of national pride in the French and English is irksome and loathsome to those of us who are not French or English. And since civilization and good manners demand, more than anything else, that one hide any sense of one's own superiority, and any contempt for the people one is dealing with, however reasonable and well founded those feelings might be, you would think that the French and English ought to hide their attitude toward foreigners. The English don't pride themselves on their good manners; rather, they pride themselves on not having any, or on having bad manners: so their behavior will hardly surprise us. But the French not only pride themselves on such manners, but want to be, believe themselves to be, and definitely are, the best-educated people in the world. In fact their sense of their own superiority largely depends on this. So it seems strange that when speaking or writing to foreigners, even the best mannered of Frenchmen can't stop himself, or it just doesn't occur to him to stop himself, from making them aware in some way or other (but clearly) that he considers them indisputably inferior to himself. And greatly inferior when it comes to what they write.

The whole situation is even stranger if one remembers how worried and sensitive the French are about seeming ridiculous. Because if their pretension seems ridiculous to someone like myself who finds it well founded and actually useful and admirable, how much more ridiculous must it seem to people who don't think it so well founded or who find it absolutely unfounded and excessive, etc.?

Animals. They Give Everything — Desperation — Children — Reflection. Lack of Reflection — Hope — Memories of My Life

Unarmed, a man fighting an animal of the same size and strength as himself—a big dog, for example—is unlikely to come out on top, and most probably will lose. To win he needs a weapon, thus acquiring a strength beyond nature and a definite superiority. The reason for this is that the dog puts everything into it, the whole of itself, goes beyond his capacities even, while the man always holds back from the action quite a large part of himself, and always does less than he might. The dog doesn't consider the danger, doesn't think, doesn't deploy any prudence. The man does the opposite, unless absolutely desperate, a state he hardly ever reaches, even when there would be every reason to. He always holds back, because he always goes on hoping; and holding back like this he doesn't achieve what he hoped he would, or doesn't escape what he hoped to escape; the very things that he would have achieved, would have escaped, if he hadn't hoped. That this is really the reason for his losing out, you can see watching children, who are far more likely than adults to come out even or on top in a fight with an animal of equal strength to their own, and will sometimes actually start such fights themselves. The adolescent, and even more so the younger child, puts his whole self into it, like the animal, or almost. This is why I can't see anything implausible in the story of the baby Hercules strangling the two snakes. I think it's more likely to be true than the one of the adult Hercules tearing the Nemean lion to pieces with his bare hands, once again unarmed, as in the previous fight with the snakes.

Compassion for the Dead—Consolation—Immortality of the Soul—Death—Memories of My Life

One of people's arguments for the immortality of the soul is that everybody agrees about it. My own feeling is that one could use the same argument and agreement against immortality, and with more reason, in that the emotion I'm going to talk about springs directly from nature and not from opinions, reasoning, or traditions; that is to say, it's a pure feeling and not an opinion. If man is immortal why do we weep over the dead? Nature has given all of us this impulse to weep over the death of our loved ones, and in weeping for them not to think of ourselves, but of the person who has died; of all the weeping people do, this is the least self-centered. People who are in some way seriously damaged by someone's death but don't have any other reason to be upset by it do not weep, and if they do they're not thinking of their own losses at all while weeping. We really are moved by the dead. Naturally, unthinkingly, or before thinking and despite thinking, we feel they are unhappy, we pity them, we consider them wretched, and their death a calamity. It was the same for the ancients who considered it absolutely inhuman to speak ill of the dead and offend their memory; and their wise men ruled that one mustn't insult either the wretched or the dead, referring to the wretched and the dead together as if alike. Same again with the moderns, same with all men; so it always was and always will be. But why pity the dead, why reckon them unhappy if their souls are immortal? When someone weeps over another who has died, he isn't moved by the thought that that person is in a place or state of punishment; in that case he couldn't weep for him; he'd hate him, because he'd feel he was wicked. Or at least the grief would be mixed with horror and disgust; and everyone knows from experience that the grief we feel for the dead isn't mixed with horror or disgust and isn't roused by this thought, nor is it even remotely of this kind. What then does our compassion for the dead come from if not from our believing, in response to an inmost feeling, without thinking, that they have lost their life, lost their being; conditions that, again without reasoning, despite reason in fact, we naturally believe are good, and their loss bad? So we don't naturally believe in the immortality of the soul; on the contrary, we believe that the dead really are dead and not alive, and that someone who is dead no longer exists.

But if we believe this, why weep for the dead? How can one pity someone who no longer exists? We weep for the dead, not insofar as dead, but as they were alive; we weep over the person that was alive, and who in life was dear to us, and we weep over him because he has ceased to live, because he is not living now and doesn't exist. What grieves us is not that he is suffering anything now, but that he has suffered this last and irreparable calamity (as we see it) of being deprived of life and being. It is this calamity that has *befallen* him that is the cause and the object of our compassion and our weeping; as for the present, we weep for his memory, not for him.

Upbringing. Teaching—Children. Social Machiavellianism—Hatred of Our Peers— Memories of My Life

Seeing themselves in the mirror and imagining there is another creature there just like themselves drives animals mad, provokes a fury of extreme pain. See, for example, the monkey in Pougens's story "Joco," in *Nuovo Ricoglitore*, Milan, March 1827, pp. 215–216. The same thing happens with our own small children. See Roberti's "Letter of a 16-Month-Old Boy." What great love toward our peers nature instills in us!!*

> *I myself saw a very tame pet canary get angry with his own image as soon as a mirror was placed in front of him and fly at it with arched wings and beak raised.

Physiognomy. Eyes—Youth—Inspiring Others— Old Age—Memories of My Life

It's sad indeed when a man reaches the moment when he feels he can no longer inspire anyone else. Man's great desire, the great drive behind his actions, words, looks, and bearing right up to old age is his desire to inspire, to communicate something to his spectators and audience.

Moral Etiquette—Social Machiavellianism— Modesty—Self-Esteem—Memories of My Life

The love and esteem a literary man has for literature or a scientist for science are often in inverse proportion to the love and esteem each has for himself.

Pleasure, Theory of—Memories—Vagueness—Handbook
of Practical Philosophy—Memories of My Life

Memories of My Life. Having changed where I've lived fairly often, staying months or years, more or less, in this place and that, I realized I was never happy, never centered, never really at home in any place, however fine in other respects it might be, until I had memories that attached themselves to the place, to the rooms where I was living, to the streets, the houses I visited; memories that amounted to nothing more than being able to say, I was here some long while ago, and here, many months ago now, I did, saw, or heard this or that, something maybe quite unimportant, but the memory, the being able to remember it, made it important and sweet to me. Obviously, I could hardly arrive at this ability to tap a rich store of memories related to the places I lived in until some time had passed, and equally obviously, with time I was bound to arrive at it. So wherever I went, I was always sad the first months and then as time passed I always found I had grown happy and attached to whatever place it was. With memory it had almost become my birth place.

Compassion—Compassion, Charity—Upbringing.
Teaching—Youth—Human Unhappiness (Proofs of)—
Old Age—Memories of My Life

The truly and perfectly compassionate person doesn't exist. Young people ought to be more capable of compassion than others, when they're in the bloom of youth, when everything is still a delight for them, when they don't suffer at all, because even if they have some reason for suffering they don't feel it. On the other hand, not having suffered, young people don't know enough about human unhappiness, they think of it almost as an illusion, or real but happening in another world, because their eyes are full of happiness. Someone suffering is not capable of compassion. The only person perfectly placed to feel compassion would be someone who has suffered, but is now not suffering at all and is in full possession of his physical health and faculties. But the only people who enjoy such a physical state and aren't suffering at all are young people, and they haven't suffered in the past. Even if nothing else goes wrong, the loss of youth is a blow for everyone, though one feels this the more to the extent to which one has been spared other troubles. Past twenty-five every man is aware of one very bitter blow: the decline of his body, the withering of the bloom of his days, the dwindling and irretrievable loss of his beloved youth.

Compassion, Charity—Upbringing. Teaching—Interest in Others—Self-Sacrifice—Memories of My Life

The first precondition for sacrificing yourself or doing things for others is self-esteem and having a high opinion of yourself; this because the first precondition for acting on behalf of others is having high hopes for yourself.

TRANSLATOR'S NOTE

Leopardi was himself a practiced translator, and in line with the *Zibaldone*'s constant attention to language, or rather languages, he includes the word "translation" in his index and lists twenty-seven entries that deal with the subject: one of the first immediately positions translation within the force field—one of the book's dominant themes—that sets a detached, manipulative intellect in conflict with emotion and spontaneity:

> There's no doubt that what is most beautiful in the arts and in writing comes from nature and not from studying or affectation. But a translator is obliged to use affectation; I mean he has to struggle to express himself in someone else's style and personality and to repeat what another person said after that person's fashion and manner. So you can see how unlikely it is that fine literature is going to be well translated, since a good translation would inevitable be made up of properties that jar with each other and seem incompatible and contradictory. Likewise the mind, spirit, and capacities of the translator. This is especially true when one of the main qualities of the original consists in its being not affected but natural and

spontaneous, something the translator of his very nature cannot be.

Certainly one of the first problems the translator faces in the *Zibaldone* is that the voice is uninhibited and spontaneous to the point of impatience, piling up clauses one on top of another in Leopardi's habitual sense of scandal at the distance between reality and received wisdom. Some sentences are monstrously long and bizarrely assembled, shifting from formal rhetorical structures to the most flexible use of apposition, juxtaposition, inference, and implication, the whole being liberally peppered with abbreviations, foreign terms, and et ceteras. It is also an eccentric voice, if only because in the early nineteenth century "proper" Italian was spoken and written by fewer than five percent of Italians, and of course Leopardi's Italian had been overwhelmingly learned from books, mainly old books, largely foreign books, his range of personal acquaintance, at least in the early and most prolific years of the diary, being drastically limited to his family's circle of friends in the fairly remote and backward town of Recanati. Most of all, though, this is a voice under strain, working at the limit of the writer's youthful mental powers as he seeks to turn intuition and reflection into a history of the human psyche, often using his own shorthand terms and constantly latching onto any syntax that comes his way, old or new, to keep the argument moving forward. In general, reading this prose, even a native speaker, let alone an English translator, will find it almost impossible to separate out what is the standard language of the time, what the deliberately archaic, what the idiosyncratic, and so on.

In addition to this personal, urgent spoken flavor—something absolutely essential for both our enjoyment and understanding of the author's ideas—there is nevertheless the fact that the *Zibaldone* is also a scientific text, an immense work of anthropology, psychology, and philosophy, in which accurate and consistent use of terminology is of the essence. Here matters are made more problematic by the fact that over the years Leopardi himself alters the sense he gives to some key words as his understanding of his subject deepens; *amor proprio*, for example (self-love or self-regard), which at the beginning of the work is more or less synonymous with *egoismo* (egoism, selfishness, self-centeredness), is gradually but in the end emphatically distinguished from it, self-regard now being seen positively as an essential precondition of any kind of project or enthusiasm, while egoism becomes the automatic, crass, unthinking, and selfish protection of one's own interests and safety, a quality more associated with fear and retreat than with hope and openness.

Meantime a word like "illusion," which at the beginning of the book might seem to have the meaning that we would normally attribute to it, of something incorrect and ingenuous, a false projection, an error to be put aside as soon as possible, soon takes on its more characteristic "Leopardian" sense of "that sort of belief or enthusiasm or hope" that allows us to act as if life had some meaning and purpose: hence love between man and woman is an "illusion"; likewise Christianity, religion, beliefs of all kinds, patriotism, and friendship. In general an illusion, for Leopardi, is something worth cultivating and sustaining, a spring for positive action, even if this means deliberately fooling oneself and being less lucid than one might be. Indeed, to understand Leopardi's use of the word "illusion" and its changing validity in different periods of the human psyche's development is to understand his sense of the pathos of the modern human condition, on the one hand bent on applying reason to destroy illusion, and on the other in desperate need of some principle to give it a sense of purpose; except that in a meaningless world any such principle could only be, as Leopardi sees it, an "illusion."

Yet if, as translator, one should decide to be guided above all by the criterion of accuracy, by a search for the absolute, academic, scientific equivalent of all the terms used, as if the only thing that mattered were the semantics of the debate, Leopardi himself warns of the dangers:

> Exactness [in translation] does not necessarily mean faithfulness, etc., and another language loses its character and dies in yours, if yours, in receiving it, loses its character, something that can happen even if none of your language's grammatical rules have been broken.

Hence style and voice, and likewise the play between individual voice and common language, are both crucial to Leopardi.

> Perfect translation consists in this, that the translated author does not seem, for example, Greek in Italian or French in German, but the same in Italian or German as he is in Greek or French. This is what's difficult and not possible in all languages. . . . In German it's easy to translate in such a way that an author is Greek, Latin, Italian, or French in German, but not so that he is the same in German as he was in his lan-

guage. He can never be that in the language of translation,
if he stays Greek, French, etc. In which case the translation,
however accurate, is not a translation, because the author is
not like that, I mean doesn't sound, for example, to the Germans the way he does to the Greeks or French, and doesn't
produce in German readers more or less the same effect he
produces in the French readers.

So, the translator approaching the *Zibaldone* finds himself
obliged to be semantically precise—otherwise the subtlety of the
debate Leopardi is engaged in will be lost—but attentive too to the
shifting meaning of the terms as the diary progresses; at the same
time he is encouraged to reproduce, mimic, or "affect" (to use Leopardi's term) the vitality and excitement of the text, which is itself
an enactment of the tension between intellect and emotion, a tension that forms such a large part of the book's subject matter; and
finally he must try to do all this in such a way that Leopardi's voice
has the same sound to an English ear as it does to an Italian.

This last injunction simply cannot be respected. Leopardi's
idiosyncratic use of language will always have a very special flavor
to Italians, coming as it does just before the country's unification
and the systematic linguistic standardization that was gradually
imposed in the second half of the nineteenth century. All Italian schoolchildren study a little Leopardi, and for all of them that
voice is absolutely individual and memorable, in part for the particular way it orders the words in the sentence and then again for
its creation of a curiously intimate atmosphere of archaism, something achieved, curiously enough, without actually referring back,

whether lexically or syntactically, to any previous use of the Italian language that ever was. A translator can hint at these idiosyncrasies and curiosities, but he or she simply cannot reproduce the full effect of this highly individual author on his fellow native speakers.

At the practical level, paragraph by paragraph one is looking at questions like, Do I keep the page-long sentences as they are, or do I break them up? Do I make the book more immediately comprehensible for English readers than it is for present-day Italians (for whom footnotes giving a modern Italian paraphrase are sometimes necessary), ideally aligning the reading experience with that of the original text's contemporary readers (though actually there were no contemporary readers since the *Zibaldone* was not published until long after Leopardi's death)? Above all, do I allow all the writer's Latinisms—most but not all entirely standard in Italian—to come through in the English, using words of Latin origin, something that would inevitably give the prose a more formal, austere feel, or do I go for Anglo-Saxon monosyllables and phrasal verbs to get across the work's curiously excited intimacy?

Here, for example, is a brief and by Leopardi's standards very simple entry on hope and suicide.

La speranza non abbandona mai l'uomo in quanto alla natura. Bensì in quanto alla ragione. Perciò parlano stoltamente quelli che dicono (gli autori della *Morale universelle* t. 3.) che il suicidio non possa seguire senza una specie di pazzia, essendo impossibile senza questa il rinunziare alla speranza ec. Anzi tolti i sentimenti religiosi, è una felice e naturale, ma vera e continua pazzia, il seguitar sempre a

sperare, e a vivere, ed è contrarissimo alla ragione, la quale ci
mostra troppo chiaro che non v'è speranza nessuna per noi.

Was I to write this?

Hope never abandons man in relation to his nature, but in
relation to his reason. So people (the authors of *La morale
universelle*, vol. 3) are stupid when they say suicide can't be
committed without a kind of madness, it being impossible to
renounce all hope without it. Actually, having set aside religious sentiments, always to go on hoping is a felicitous and
natural, though true and continuous, madness and totally
contrary to reason which shows too clearly that there is no
hope for any of us.

Or, alternatively:

Men never lose hope in response to nature, but in response
to reason. So people (the authors of the *Morale universelle*,
vol. 3) who say no one can kill himself without first sinking
into madness, since in your right mind you never lose hope,
have got it all wrong. Actually, leaving religious belief out of
the equation, our going on hoping and living is a happy, natural, but also real and constant madness, and something quite
contrary to reason, which all too clearly shows that there is no
hope for any of us.

Or some mixture of the two? The fact is that while I find it hard to
imagine anyone translating Dante's famous *Lasciate ogni speranza*
any other way than "Abandon all hope" (curiously introducing this

rather heavy verb "abandon" where in the Italian we have a simple *lasciare*, to leave), here I just can't imagine any reason for not reorganizing *La speranza non abbandona mai l'uomo* into "Man never loses hope." This because when, after thirty-three years in Italy, I read Leopardi today, he seems, despite the almost two hundred years that separate us, to be speaking urgently and informally, albeit with his bookish background and an elegance that has become second nature.

All of these questions relating to approach and style, many of them typical of any translation project, but some of them absolutely specific to Leopardi and the *Zibaldone*, were, in the case of this particular translation, unexpectedly complicated by the fact that just as I got down to work a team of seven translators and two specialist editors based in Birmingham, England, published the first unabridged and fully annotated English edition of the *Zibaldone*, a simply enormous task. So now there was the further question of whether I should look at their version before starting mine, after finishing, or not at all.

Well, it only makes sense after finishing a difficult translation to check another version of the same text if there is one; there is no point in publishing something with straightforward semantic errors if these can be avoided by looking at someone else's efforts. On the other hand, there would equally be no point in my producing a translation that was merely an echo of theirs.

In the event I decided to look at the Translator's Note in the new edition and a few parts of the translation that did not correspond to the extracts I was translating, just to get a sense of how they had dealt with the various issues of style. Immediately I realized that these translators had faced a greater dilemma than I did. Seven translators and two editors would each have heard Leopardi's voice and responded to his singular project, his particular brand of despair, in their own several ways; but one can't publish a text with seven (or nine) different voices. Strategies must have been agreed upon, and a single editor must ultimately have gone through all two thousand–plus pages to even things out. This no doubt meant establishing a standard voice that all the translators could write toward and making certain decisions across the board, particularly with respect to key words, the overall register, lexical fields, and so on. In any event, after reading a few random paragraphs of the translation itself, I felt reassured that my work would not merely be a duplication of theirs, if only because I heard the text quite differently than they did.

As I had expected, the Birmingham translation, if I can call it that, proved immensely useful to me, at the checking stage, after I had completed a first draft of my own version, in that it did indeed save me making a number of mistakes. In this respect I had a considerable advantage over them since vice versa a consideration of my translation would have saved them some mistakes. A translation of this kind is immensely complex, and no one is so accurate and perfect that he cannot gain from comparing notes with another person who has covered the territory. I am immensely grateful to have had the chance to see their work. My version is definitely the better for it.

However, what most struck me when finally I read the corresponding passages of the Birmingham translation—produced, as I said, by seven different translators—was the absolute uniqueness of each reading response, which is the inevitable result, I suppose, of the individual background each of us brings to a book, all the reading and writing and listening and talking we've done in the past, our particular interests, beliefs, and obsessions. I hear Leopardi in an English that has a completely different tone and feel from the one my colleagues have collectively aimed at. I just hear a different man speaking to me—a different voice, in particular a voice that looks forward in its tone and insistence and sheer, raw energy to such writers as Gadda, Beckett, Bernhard, and Cioran, men who very largely shared Leopardi's lively, corrosive pessimism and profound sense of irony.

Here is a passage where voice seems crucial.

Dido, *Aeneid* 4, 659 ff.
> *Moriemur inultae,*
> *Sed moriamur, ait. Sic sic iuvat ire sub umbras.*

Virgilio volle qui esprimere (fino e profondo sentimento, e degno di un uomo conoscitore de' cuori, ed esperto delle passioni e delle sventure, come lui) quel piacere che l'animo prova nel considerare e rappresentarsi non solo vivamente, ma minutamente, intimamente, e pienamente la sua disgrazia, i suoi mali; nell'esagerarli, anche, a se stesso, se può (che se può, certo lo fa), nel riconoscere, o nel figurarsi, ma certo persuadersi e proccurare con ogni sforzo di persuadersi fermamente, ch'essi sono eccessivi, senza fine, senza limiti, senza rimedio nè impedimento nè compenso nè consolazione veruna possibile, senza alcuna circostanza che gli alleggerisca; nel vedere insomma e sentire vivacemente che la sua sventura è propriamente immensa e perfetta e quanta può essere per tutte le parti, e precluso e ben serrato ogni adito o alla speranza o alla consolazione qualunque, in maniera che l'uomo resti propriamente solo colla sua intera sventura. Questi sentimenti si provano negli accessi di disperazione, nel gustare il passeggero conforto del pianto, (dove l'uomo si piglia piacere a immaginarsi più infelice che può), talvolta anche nel primo punto e sentimento o novella ec. del suo male ec.

We start with a quotation from the *Aeneid*. Leopardi assumes we know our Latin and our Latin literature. This is the moment when Carthaginian queen Dido prepares to kill herself after her lover Aeneas has deserted her. She's happy to go, she says in her despair. Then, from this rather scholarly opening, Leopardi sets out to describe a particular psychological state, a particular passion if you like: the pleasure that can be taken in savoring extremities of desperation. Even those who don't know any Italian will see at a glance that most of the paragraph is made up of a single sentence, broken up with a couple of parentheses and laden with repetitive elements, mainly adverbs, that accumulate to create a sense of insistence — *vivamente, ma minutemente, intimamente, e pienamente*, or again, *senza fine, senza limiti, senza rimedio nè impedimento nè compenso nè consolazione*. While the first elements in these lists are correctly divided by commas, the later ones are not, suggesting an acceleration, an increase in excitement. A brutally literal translation of the passage would give:

Dido, *Aeneid* 4, 659 ff.

"I shall die unavenged, but let me die—she says—thus, thus, it pleases to go down among the shades."

Virgil wanted here to express (subtle and deep emotion, and worthy of a man who knows hearts, and an expert in passions and misfortunes, like him) that pleasure that the mind feels in considering and representing to itself not only vivaciously, but in detail, intimately, and fully its downfall, its ills; in exaggerating them, even, to itself, if it can (which if it can, certainly it does), in the recognizing, or in the imagining, but certainly the persuading itself and arranging with every effort to persuade itself steadfastly, that they are excessive, without end, without limit, without remedy or impediment or reward or consolation of any possible kind, without any circumstance that lightens them; in seeing in short and vivaciously feeling that its misfortune is really immense and perfect and as great as can be in all parts, and closed and locked every entry either to hope or to consolation whatever, in a manner that the man remains really alone with his entire misfortune. These feelings are felt in bursts of desperation, in savoring the passing comfort of crying (where man gets the pleasure of imagining himself more unhappy than he can be), sometimes even at the first moment and feeling or news, etc., of his ill, etc.

Such a rendering indicates that this is hardly a difficult passage from the point of view of comprehension. And in the end although many sections of the *Zibaldone* are indeed very difficult to understand, if only because Leopardi was writing more for himself than for the public, all the same, when, whether alone or with the help of others, one has figured out the original, the real difficulty is only beginning: that of expressing the content in an English that does justice to the Italian. Here the cumulative power, and insistence of the text seems at once to participate in the extremity of the emotions felt, but by that very extremity to suggest that there is a certain comedy in this engagement with one's own unhappiness, a certain element of the grotesque. It is as if on the one hand Leopardi acknowledged the nobility of Dido, the sublimity of Virgil—such emotions made sense in this context where the illusions of heroism and nobility were still felt—while at the same time pointing out the absurdity of this pleasure we take in exaggerating our troubles, and here he seems to look forward to the torment and writhing of the speaker in *Notes from Underground* or Beckett's Hamm, who opens *Endgame* with the complacent reflection, "Can there be misery . . . loftier than mine?" The passage, that is, vibrates between past and present, ambiguously admiring the same emotion in one period and allowing it to appear almost fatuous in another.

The problem for the translator is that while structures like "representing to itself" are possible in English, they seem unusual and rather intellectual, whereas this is fairly standard Italian even today. This quandary comes up again and again: it is possible to offer an almost literal translation of much of what Leopardi writes and indeed to use a large number of cognates from the Latin, but this does not give a sense of the persuasive rhythms behind the original; rather, it produces exactly that "Italian in English" which Leopardi warned against. Nor does such an approach always give quite the sense: for example, where Leopardi describes Virgil as a *conoscitore* (literally, "knower") of hearts and an *esperto* in passions, in my literal translation I have given "expert." But is this really the exact sense here? An expert—the word used as noun rather than adjective—is someone you consult for special advice, a person with a role in human relations or the world of work, but "esperto" in Italian also has the more basic sense of someone with experience of the territory, not a TV pundit.

Again, a word like *sfortuna* is absolutely standard in contemporary Italian—someone has some small, or very large, mishap and you say, *Che sfortuna*—but hardly used in daily English, where one would not say "What a misfortune!" if someone lost his wallet or fell to his death from a cliff. On the other hand, it's quite possible that the usage was a lot more common in English in the 1820s, when this book was written. Does this mean I should use it because appropriately archaic? But if one accepted this reasoning, one would have to translate the whole work in the style of the 1820s, and even if that were possible (and for me it would definitely not be), would such an approach make sense when one thinks that English was at a completely different stage of development then than was Italian, the distance from the English of, say, Jane Austen to modern English being quite different in its intensity and nature from the difference between Leopardi and modern Italian? Not to mention the fact that looking for a pastiche of early-nineteenth-century English would increase the element of affectation that Leopardi felt ran contrary to the life of a text.

In any event, this is how my colleagues who worked on the Birmingham translation gave the passage, a version I didn't see until I was at the checking stage of my own work.

"I will die unavenged,
But let me die, she said. Thus, thus it pleases me to go among
the shades."

Virgil here wished to express (a subtle and profound
feeling, worthy of a connoisseur of hearts, an expert in passions and misfortunes, like him) that pleasure which the soul
feels in examining and portraying its troubles, its ills, not only
vividly but minutely, intimately, and fully; even in exaggerating them to itself, if it can (and if it can, certainly it does), in
recognizing, or imagining, but certainly persuading itself, and
striving with every effort to persuade itself firmly, that they
are extreme and without end, without limits, without remedy
or impediment or compensation or any possible consolation, that there is no circumstance that could lighten them;
in seeing, in short, and feeling keenly that its tribulations
are immense and total and as terrible as can be, in all their
elements, and that every approach to hope or consolation
is barred and shut, in such a way that a man remains truly
alone with his entire misfortune. These feelings are experienced during attacks of despair, in tasting the fleeting comfort of tears (where a man takes pleasure in imagining himself
to be as unhappy as possible), and sometimes even at the first
moment and sensation or news, etc., of his misfortune, etc.

As I said, I owe a great deal to the Birmingham translation in
that it offered me the possibility of checking my work against someone else's, questioning my own decisions, usually on issues of comprehension, very rarely on issues of voice and style. Here, for ex-

ample, comparing with my own version I had to ask myself whether this translation was right to use "connoisseur" and "expert," which give the sense that Virgil is, as it were, a collector or consultant. Connoisseur in particular, it seems to me, has a very limited and specific area of use—fine arts, wines, an aesthetic, detached attitude—which is hardly the case with the generic *conoscitore*. Dante, we remember, referred to Virgil as *Tu duca, tu segnore, e tu maestro*, suggesting more the idea of a spiritual guide than a connoisseur. And is there any need to include the rather clumsy "like him" at the end of the parenthesis—"an expert in passions and misfortunes, like him"—when we know perfectly well we are referring to him? Or if we want to keep the reinforcement, mightn't it be more fluent to write, "expert as he was in passions and misfortunes"?

Other words that create some unease for me here are "portraying" for *rapprensentarsi* (which means specifically "picturing something for oneself," not describing it for others), and in particular "terrible" for Leopardi's *perfetto*. What does it mean that someone's troubles are "perfect"? Presumably we are returning to the root sense of the word, the idea of something complete, finished, absolutely done, something to which nothing more can be added. I suspect there is an irony here, Leopardi noting how the completeness of the suffering, its having reached its "perfection," becomes a source of perverse self-congratulation on the part of the sufferer. So this might be one case where one ought to keep the Latin cognate and allow it to appear in English in all its provocative oddness: the mind's sufferings are "perfect."

But more generally, when I look at this translation, or indeed so many translations from Italian, I wonder whether the sort of musty tone established by bringing together groups of words like "misfortune," "ills" (for the standard and common Italian *mali*), "impediment" (for *impedimento*), "tribulations" (for *sfortuna*) doesn't put a distance between us and the text, a distance that is not there in the Italian, where all the words used in this passage form part of ordinary standard contemporary Italian conversation. Then, aside from the choice of the particular words, there is the question of creating a cohering fluency and urgency that would allow the translation to express the punch that it gradually gathers in the Italian.

In any event, here is the version that I was checking against theirs.

I shall die unavenged, but let me die — she says — like this, like this, it's good to go down among the shades.

Here Virgil wanted to get across (and it's a deep, subtle sentiment, worthy of a man who knew the human heart and had experience of passion and tragedy) the pleasure the mind takes in dwelling on its downfall, its adversities, then picturing them for itself, not just intensely, but minutely, intimately, completely; in exaggerating them even, if it can (and if it can, it certainly will), in recognizing, or imagining, but definitely in persuading itself and making absolutely sure it persuades itself, beyond any doubt, that these adversities are extreme, endless, boundless, irremediable, unstoppable, beyond any redress, or any possible consolation, bereft of any circumstance that might lighten them; in short in seeing and intensely feeling that its own personal tragedy is truly immense and perfect and as complete as it could be in all its parts, and that every door toward hope and consolation of any kind has been shut off and locked tight, so that now he is quite alone with his tragedy, all of it. These are feelings that come in moments of intense desperation as one savors the fleeting comfort of tears (when you take pleasure supposing yourself as unhappy as you can ever be), sometimes even at the first moment, the first emotion, on hearing the news, etc., that spells disaster, etc.

Coming back to a translation of some months before and looking at it with a certain detachment, one almost always finds cause to object. I too have used different words for *sfortuna* (in particular I have risked using "tragedy," not in its strictly technical sense, but in the colloquial way we all use it — but this is a tragedy!), I too have introduced commas where perhaps they might have been left out, and so on. But my policy throughout the translation was to allow for "English-sounding" formulas to mesh with the semantics of the original, to do everything possible to make Leopardi English in English (one needn't worry, some distant echoes of Italian will always remain): so we have "the pleasure the mind takes in dwelling on its downfall, its adversities" allowing the persuasive alliteration of the d's in a typically abrupt English structure of subject-verb-object, where the literal translation of the Italian gives: "that pleasure that the mind feels in considering and representing to itself not only vivaciously, but in detail, intimately, and fully its downfall, its ills." My version then recovers the rest of the material in the original by using the pronoun "them" to make the downfall and the adversities an object of the second verb "picturing":

the pleasure the mind takes in dwelling on its downfall, its adversities, then picturing them for itself, not just intensely, but minutely, intimately, completely . . .

My belief is that the semantic nuance of the original can be kept, and likewise the fluency *and* the syntactical complexity, if one is willing to reorganize everything, to think and rethink and write and rewrite. "Endless, boundless, irremediable, unstoppable" seems to me more effective than a literal rendering "without end, without limit, without remedy or impediment." Another example would be "that every door toward hope and consolation of any kind has been shut off and locked tight, so that now he is quite alone with his tragedy, all of it," where the literal rendering is "and closed and locked every entry either to hope or to consolation whatever, in a manner that the man remains really alone with his entire misfortune." What is at stake of course is readability, and although one would never want to sacrifice subtlety of thought for ease of reading, it is also true that if a long text seems stylistically clumsy and incompetent, it begins to lose authority and credibility. Italians will always read Leopardi, however arduous, because he is a mainstay of their culture, a figure whose influence on the writers and poets of the twentieth century was simply enormous. English speakers will read him if he seems worth reading, and not otherwise.

In any event, the more I worked over this translation, which turned out to be by far the most challenging I have ever tackled, the more I came to the conclusion that, beyond the duty of semantic accuracy (which always remains), all I had to do (all!) was to sit down, for a few hundred hours, and perform this Leopardi—in the way that seemed most right, most authentically close to the tone and the feel of it at the moment of my translating (since every translation would be somewhat different if we had done it a month before, or a month later, or even an hour); just to hear the text and experience it absolutely as intensely as I could, allowing myself, which fortunately was not difficult, to fall into Leopardi's caustic way of thinking about things, then to express this in English, perform it in English, *my* English, not an affected, pastiched nineteenth-century English, as he performed it, sitting at his desk, writing in Italian, his very peculiar and special Italian. The falseness of affectation, I decided, which Leopardi felt was inevitable in any translation, could at least to some extent be overcome by a more than willing affinity, an even perverse identification, with his project, my passion for his pessimistic *Passions*. In this regard it's worth noting that I undertook this translation—a rare privilege—not, as alas so often in the past, because I needed or even wanted the work, quite the contrary, I did not want the work, I already had far too much work, but out of a lasting admiration, sympathy, attraction, call it what you will, to Leopardi. I was glad, on signing the contract, to think that I would be sitting beside Leopardi for a few months. And I firmly believe that this state of affairs changes the way we work. Leopardi himself, in a period of depression, wrote that "only poets inspire in me a burning desire to translate and take hold of what I read." The *Zibaldone* is not poetry, but Leopardi is certainly a writer who rouses that excitement in me to take hold of the text and put it before the reader with the intensity I feel when reading it.

Toward the end of this selection, Leopardi writes:

It's sad indeed when a man reaches the moment when he feels he can no longer inspire anyone else. Man's great desire, the great drive behind his actions, words, looks, and bearing right up to old age is his desire to inspire, to communicate something to his spectators and audience.

It seems clear that he felt he was arriving at that point. But his very ability to express the idea proved him wrong. The translator's task throughout this work is to go on proving him wrong, to go on showing that Leopardi's thought is still a source of inspiration and excitement.

This page constitutes a continuation of the copyright page on p. iv.

Library of Congress Cataloging-in-Publication Data
Leopardi, Giacomo, 1798–1837, author.
[Zibaldone. English]
Passions / Giacomo Leopardi ; translated by Tim Parks.
    pages   cm. — (The Margellos World Republic of Letters)
Summary: "Revenge — Revenge is so sweet one often wishes to be insulted so as to
be able to take revenge, and I don't mean just by an old enemy, but anyone, or even
(especially when in a really bad mood) by a friend." — from *Passions*

"The extraordinary quality of Giacomo Leopardi's writing and the innovative nature
of his thought were never fully recognized in his lifetime. *Zibaldone*, his 4,500-page
intellectual diary — a vast collection of thoughts on philosophy, civilization, literary
criticism, linguistics, humankind and its vanities, and other varied topics — remained
unpublished until more than a half-century after his death. But shortly before he died,
Leopardi began to organize a small, thematic collection of his writings in an attempt
to give structure and system to his philosophical musings. Now freshly translated into
English by master translator, novelist, and critic Tim Parks, Leopardi's *Passions* presents
164 entries reflecting the full breadth of human passion. The volume offers a fascinating
introduction to Leopardi's arguments and insights, as well as a glimpse of the concerns
of thinkers to come, among them Nietzsche, Dostoyevsky, Wittgenstein, Gadda, and
Beckett." — Provided by publisher.
ISBN 978-0-300-18633-8 (hardback)
I. Parks, Tim, translator.   II. Title.
PQ4708.Z3213 2014
858'.703 — dc23
2014006319

A catalogue record for this book is available from the British Library.

This paper meets the requirements of ANSI/NISO Z39.48-1992 (Permanence of Paper).

10 9 8 7 6 5 4 3 2 1

Giacomo Leopardi was born in 1798 in Recanati, a small town near the Adriatic coast. His father, an impoverished aristocrat, had built up a huge library where Leopardi spent much of his youth, learning many languages, establishing a reputation for precocious genius, and ruining his health, early scoliosis reducing him to the state of a hunchback. Destined by his parents for a scholarly career in the church, he rebelled to become one of Italy's finest poets and essayists, though the extraordinary quality of his writing and the innovative nature of his thought were never fully recognized in his lifetime. Increasingly disillusioned, throughout his twenties Leopardi moved between Rome, Milan, Bologna, and Florence in search of romance and an adequate income, both of which eluded him. Meantime he kept a journal, the *Zibaldone*, that would eventually run to four thousand pages, exploring philosophical positions that often look forward to Nietzsche, Wittgenstein, and twentieth-century existentialism. Profoundly pessimistic and despairing of all worldly success, in 1833 Leopardi withdrew with a close friend to Naples, where he died in 1837. The *Zibaldone* was not published until 1898. Leopardi's most famous poems include *The Infinite*, *To Silvia*, and *Broom*. The major works are the *Canti* (Songs), *Operette Morali* (Moral dialogues), and the *Zibaldone*.

Tim Parks was born in Manchester, U.K., in 1954, grew up in London, and studied at Cambridge and Harvard before moving to Italy in 1981. He is author of some fifteen novels, once short-listed and three times long-listed for the Booker Prize, as well as various works of nonfiction, including four memoirs covering aspects of life in contemporary Italy. His many translations from the Italian include works by Moravia, Tabucchi, Calvino, Calasso, and Machia-velli (*The Prince*). He has written widely on the subject of transla-tion, and his book *Translating Style* is an unusual attempt to fuse literary criticism with translation analysis. For more than a decade he has run a postgraduate degree on translation at IULM Univer-sity, Milan, and he is a regular contributor to the *New York Review of Books* and the *London Review of Books*.